Dealing with
Difficult People
for ROOKIES

Titles in the *for* ROOKIES series

About the authors

With many years of work experience, covering politics, diplomatic service and law, **Frances Kay** has a wide range of contacts and works with organizations in the field of research and corporate development. Frances coaches, trains and advises on all aspects of personal and career development and professional relationship building. An experienced author, she has had twenty business books published, including *New Kid on the Block* and *Hello, I Must Be Going: the wallflower's guide to networking*, and *Time & Stress Management for Rookies*, all published by Marshall Cavendish.

Dealing with Difficult People

for ROOKIES

Copyright © 2010 LID Editorial Empresarial and Marshall Cavendish International

First published in 2010 by Marshall Cavendish Business
An imprint of Marshall Cavendish International
PO Box 65829
London EC1P 1NY
United Kingdom
info@marshallcavendish.co.uk
and
1 New Industrial Road
Singapore 536196
genrefsales@sg.marshallcavendish.com
www.marshallcavendish.com/genref

A member of **BPR**

businesspublishersroundtable.com

Marshall Cavendish is a trademark of Times Publishing Limited

Other Marshall Cavendish offices: Marshall Cavendish International (Asia) Private
Limited, 1 New Industrial Road, Singapore 536196 • Marshall Cavendish Corporation.
99 White Plains Road, Tarrytown NY 10591–9001, USA • Marshall Cavendish International
(Thailand) Co Ltd. 253 Asoke, 12th Floor, Sukhumvit 21 Road, Klongtoey Nua, Wattana,
Bangkok 10110, Thailand • Marshall Cavendish (Malaysia) Sdn Bhd, Times Subang, Lot 46,
Subang Hi-Tech Industrial Park, Batu Tiga, 40000 Shah Alam, Selangor Darul Ehsan,
Malaysia

A CIP record for this book is available from the British Library

ISBN 978-0-462-09978-1

Illustrations by Nuria Aparicio and Joan Guardiet

Printed and bound in Singapore by Fabulous Printers Pte Ltd

Contents

Introduction

"We must learn to live together as brothers
or perish together as fools."
– Martin Luther King (speech at St Louis, 22 March 1964)

Harmonious relationships at work – whether with your boss, colleagues, staff, clients, customers, or suppliers – are what everyone desires. While most of us can get along reasonably well with the majority of people in the workplace, there are perhaps a few characters you'll encounter along your career path who require special handling.

Professional people know how important it is to be able to deal appropriately and successfully with others where business and career development are concerned. Despite the amazing progress of technology, which enables machines to do almost anything you want, instantly, it is still important to be able to interact well with other people. It is even more important to be able to cope when, from time to time, other people behave in a seemingly unreasonable fashion. This is an issue that concerns everyone at work at some point or other. It's not just

2

being able to communicate that is important, though of course that matters. But sometimes you require troubleshooting skills for dealing with people who could (and do) cause difficulties or who seem quite impossible to handle. While many work-related relationships run smoothly, when problems occur this can have far-reaching effects on your career, your health and your happiness.

Dealing with Difficult People for Rookies is for those who are new to their career or have recently taken a new position and want to gain an advantage over their contemporaries. But it will help anyone who would like to get on better with other people, with special emphasis on workplace relationships. Today there is much reliance on qualifications and technical experience, but if you ignore the soft skills (the ability to deal with all kinds of people) this can cause problems. A balance of technical and people skills is always best if you can achieve it. Sometimes there just isn't time (due to pressure of work) to practise building rapport with others. The less you practise, the more likely you are to encounter difficulties. You could, for instance, come up against someone in a position to influence your career progression. How do you handle them? What skills are needed to ensure they do not adversely affect your promotion prospects? This book contains advice on acquiring relationship-building skills generally, and dealing with difficult people in particular. If you are keen to progress in your chosen profession, this book should prove invaluable.

So why do workplace relationships matter? Because no matter how brilliant you are at your job, if you want to get ahead, good connections at work are essential. Task awareness is fine, and being good at your job is eminently desirable. But if you can harness this with being skilled at rapport building, you will progress further and faster than those who cannot. If you are prepared to tackle this area and get it right, you may have the opportunity to positively influence the growth and profitabil-ity of your organization and enhance your own career as well. Should you have a problem dealing with a difficult person, you will find a sol-ution more swiftly if you have some sound inter-personal skills to rely on. If you feel rather nervous about tackling this area, that is perfectly natural. You may be moving into unfamiliar territory, and navigating uncharted water can make even the most confident people rather apprehensive. Just remember – dealing with difficult people in the workplace isn't scary once you've attempted it and had a little success. Your confidence in handling tricky situations will soon increase.

At every level in any organization you are likely to come across people with whom you may have little in common – colleagues, team workers, staff, managers, directors, customers, clients, suppliers. If you can develop the skill to handle all types of personalities, both easy and difficult, you will be a huge asset to your company. Bear in mind that you may be able to accomplish tasks quickly, but dealing with people often takes time. Where people are concerned, you can't rush things. This book is designed to help you cope with difficult characters and become their ally rather than their foe. Rapport building is the core element. Armed with this skill, you will have greater confidence and progress further and faster with your career.

Dealing with Difficult People for Rookies addresses issues that are commonly found in the work environment in a user-friendly and down-to-earth way. It is simple to understand, is in an acces-sible format and uses little jargon and no management-speak. With a modern approach, it is intended to convey know-how as part of the Rookies series, which offers help to those wishing to succeed in their chosen profession.

In essence, this book focuses on the wide range of personalities you meet

4   at work. If some of your co-workers and colleagues need careful handling you will, by reading to the end of this book, have all the skills at your fingertips. You will be able to manage everyone, from the charming right down to the less-than-charming characters whom you may wish to avoid. What makes such people tick? How is it best to deal with them? How can you surmount these issues, overcome the problems and be a winner? Maybe you need to match their methods – or is it a case of playing it rough, sticking it out, using whatever devices you can manage to keep them at a distance?

The following chapters deal with a variety of issues on personality clashes in the work environment, from minor tensions to outright war. Whatever stage you have reached in your career, *Dealing with Difficult People for Rookies* is for you. The advice contained here will arm you with the skills you need to cope with situations from the normal to the outrageous. It identifies classic character types, their likely behaviour and how to prepare yourself for any encounter. It suggests ways of overcoming awkward situations you would rather not face, including rapid reaction techniques to cope with unexpected emergencies and crises. Additionally, should this be part of your career plan, it will help you rise to the top by offering smooth and subtle strategies to surmount all sorts of problems. Whether experienced or not, you will find tips and tactics to avoid personality clashes and be the one everybody wants on their side.

Dealing with Difficult People for Rookies is designed to make it possible for professional relationships to flourish, for careers to progress and for workers to develop congruent communication skills which are advantageous to everyone. It will help you to understand different types of people and work with them better, thus avoiding the conflicts and disagreements that make problems for all concerned. Harmony is what is needed to give everyone an easier life – particularly at work. If you've been involved in some workplace skirmishes, and troubleshooting skills would be an advantage, read on!

Notes

There are millions of people in the world and most of them (thank goodness) are a lot like you and me. When treated appropriately, they are pleasant, friendly, decent individuals who generally enable life to be enjoyed rather than endured. Keeping within the bounds of reasonableness, where behaviour is concerned, is probably the most important rule. It is not always easy, but by and large people manage fairly successfully. Sometimes, however, despite everyone's best endeavours, things don't go according to plan. This chapter introduces the issues we face on the occasions when dealing with others is anything but easy. It describes things to look out for when people behave unreasonably and you don't know why. There is usually a reason, but finding out what it is can be tricky.

CHAPTER 1

Relationships at work

"You can tell a lot about a fellow's character
by his way of eating jellybeans."
– Ronald Reagan (quoted in the *New York Times*, 15 January 1981)

You versus the others

Do you think you get on reasonably well with others? Are you fairly lucky in being able to conduct rational exchanges with almost everyone you meet? If so, you may wonder why an entire book is being devoted to dealing with difficult people. In fact the majority of people you encounter are probably able to get on with each other without too much trouble. But when personal encounters don't go well, does it seem to you in most cases that it is the *other* person's fault? Are they, in your opinion, being "unreasonable"? Why should their reaction be so unhelpful? Do you ever wonder what is causing it?

When describing difficult people, it is easy to label them as

8   completely unreasonable, when in fact it may be just one aspect of their behaviour that is challenging. If you can invest a little time in preventing a situation from going wrong, you won't have to pick up the pieces afterwards. It is easier to identify and deal with behavioural patterns rather than to have to handle different events over and over again.

Rookie Buster

When describing difficult people, it is easy to label them as completely unreasonable, when in fact it may be just one aspect of their behaviour that is challenging.

Think for a moment. How many difficult people do you know? Can you state where and how often they crop up? Remember that however many nice, kind and pleasant people you meet, there are a good few who fall into that other category. There are numerous grades of awkward people. They can range from being ever so slightly unhelpful, all the way to seemingly off the wall and downright impossible. The reason it helps to know how to deal with them is because these characters can (and will) appear just about anywhere. And when it's in the workplace, you can't just avoid them as you might do elsewhere.

Difficult people have the knack of making themselves evident when they are about the last thing you need. That is why being able to cope with these unmanageable types without losing your head, or balance, can be such an advantage. For starters, you will not join their ranks. Instead you will be able to glide easily past them, swan-like, unruffled and calm. Or you could stand up to them, disarm them and gain control over an otherwise unpleasant occurrence. In the process you will earn the praise and respect of your colleagues and managers as well as keeping your blood pressure and stress levels within the normal limits.

Rookie Buster

Difficult people have the knack of making themselves evident when they are about the last thing you need.

How difficult are you?

First of all, how difficult do you think you are? It may seem an odd question, but maybe you've never considered the possibility that sometimes perhaps *you* are one of "those people". You've probably bought this book because it's other people who are difficult and make your life problematic. But have you ever been awkward or a nuisance? Do you ever get cross if things don't go your way? Do you have endless patience? Would you react with irritation if you were given the wrong facts, or information that you didn't want to hear? How about if you were blamed for something that had nothing to do with you?

Some of the foregoing may be familiar territory. If you think about it, everyone has the ability to be a difficult person sometimes, just as everybody has a choice – whether to be good or bad. You can choose to be difficult (or not) if you want to. With today's pressures and stresses, that is what happens from time to time for everyone. No one is entirely blameless. Some of your encounters with so-called difficult people may in fact be triggered by your own behaviour towards them. This is fundamentally a question of attitude. Attitude is a most important consideration when looking at how to deal well and effectively with other people.

Rookie Buster

Attitude is a most important consideration when looking at how to deal well and effectively with other people.

10   *A simple question*

What sort of attitude do you prefer when encountering other people? How do you feel when you meet a new colleague? What if he gives you a smile and offers a handshake? Add to that clear eye contact, an open face, clean, neat clothing and good grooming. The overall impression is a professional one, so you'll probably be feeling quite at ease. Why so? Because what he has exhibited are all *positive* attributes.

Have you any idea why you're likely to prefer this sort of approach when meeting someone for the first time? The answer is that it is simply attractive and reassuring. The person you are meeting is enthused with positive energy, and he or she wants to present well towards you. This in turn encourages a similar response from you.

An indisputable truth is that people form a swift first impression of someone – it can be as quickly as within five seconds of meeting. You have nothing on which to judge the person apart from what you see. They may well not have had the time to say a word to you. So what of this person who's just been described above? Almost imperceptibly, you will be smiling back at them, possibly extending your hand to greet them. Why? Why will you be looking on them favourably and investing positive energy into whatever you are thinking about?

Rookie Buster

People form a swift first impression of someone – it can be as quickly as within five seconds of meeting.

You could be considering them for all sorts of different reasons.

Perhaps they are welcoming you to a new department or team, in which case you are more likely to form a favourable impression of the rest of the group and look forward to working with them, because you already feel comfortable and at ease. Or maybe you are meeting someone with whom you are thinking of working on a project outside your organization. What can be better than a good first impression? If you gain the view that here is someone you can relate to, someone who is professional, someone who you may well be able to trust, that is the sign of an open and honest person. In return, you can allow yourself to relax a little, and be warm and welcoming. The scene is then set for pleasant and rewarding exchanges.

Consider the converse situation. You meet someone who scowls at you, or avoids your gaze, doesn't make ready eye contact, and whose greeting is off-putting. Perhaps their body language is also careless; they are slouching, they look rather scruffy or they are not scrupulous about their personal hygiene. What does this all add up to? A *negative* impression. Maybe these people are unfortunate, unlucky, or simply ignorant of the impression they are giving. But what you may be thinking is that you're not looking forward to working with them, or that they could be trouble, if not immediately, then at some point in the future.

Some negative types are simply angry at the world. They are constantly imagining slights where none exist or are intended. They tend to feel insulted and undervalued, and if they are whiners, they complain about the rest of humanity getting at them or treating them unfairly. In fact, their attitude works completely the opposite way to the positive attitude shown by others. These hostile and negative characters seemingly go out of their way to make it easy for reasonable people to react negatively towards them.

If the person with this bad attitude is in a superior position to you at work, you are hardly likely to relish going in to work each day. You'll soon convince yourself that you should be looking around for another position or a transfer, or moving to another organization entirely. The same applies with a possible work colleague. The negative first impression which you gain is hardly going to encourage you to employ them, invite them to become part of your team, or do business with them. In other words you recoil from them because you feel they are just "an accident waiting to happen". And sadly, you are probably right. Why do these people make their own life so difficult? Are they foolish, ignorant or plainly hostile?

It is a fact that if you behave badly or negatively towards people, they can quite easily (and justifiably) react badly and negatively towards you. So, wherever possible, do as you would be done by. People who are optimistic, friendly and attractive will find their encounters with others mirroring themselves. They will see their own demeanour reflected in the people they meet.

Rookie Buster

If you behave negatively towards people, they can quite easily (and justifiably) react negatively towards you.

Good, bad or something in between?

The importance of attitude and attraction cannot be overemphasized. If your attitude is positive, open and attractive, the people you meet will be drawn towards you in a warm and friendly manner. Unfortunately some people do seem to be born difficult, while others may become difficult because of circumstances. Then there are the fundamentally reasonable people who are made difficult by the way in which they are treated by others, the unreasonable ones. Reasonableness, politeness and good manners should be the norm. Deal with others in the best and most positive way you can. If you don't, you are likely to find yourself in trouble one way or another, sooner or later.

Although this book is written primarily for those who want to get on better with the people they encounter at work, the advice is generally applicable outside the workplace as well. Getting on with others is an essential social skill, which everyone should try to learn as early as possible. The better and more successful you become at dealing with

others, the greater the chances of smoothing your own path through   13
life, and also making things a lot easier for those around you.

Rookie Buster

Getting on with others is an essential social skill.

Relating well to other people

Many people relate well to others quite easily. But if you find it difficult
or awkward, what is the solution? The answer is to develop curiosity.
If you are interested in other people, you will get on far better with
them than if you try to be interesting yourself.

Rookie Buster

If you are interested in other people, you will get on far
better with them than if you try to be interesting yourself.

Can you remember how you learned to keep your balance when
riding a bike? Did you learn to skate or swim as a child? Are you able
to snowboard or water-ski? What was the learning process like? You
learned by observation, by watching other people, and by being shown
the way by someone proficient. Then you took a few tentative steps or
made a few wobbly attempts, and fell over again and again or sank
beneath the surface a good few times. You eventually learned by experience and by paying attention to others.

If you take the same approach towards dealing with difficult or
negative people, success will follow. Despite the millions of different
people there are around, some of them will seem familiar to you. They

14 will have characteristics, attributes and personality traits that will remind you of others you have met or engaged with. However nervous you are, if you have the courage to keep on trying, you will succeed. You will overcome your fear of stepping into the unknown, the unfamiliar, the frightening.

Types to look out for

There are lots of difficult people in the workplace, but some of the more common varieties are listed below. They come in all shapes and sizes and in varying degrees of complexity. But they all have one thing in common – they display negative behavioural traits. There's not much positive conduct to be found here, however hard you look. How best to deal with them is what follows later in the book, but to start off with, you need to be able to recognize the following types.

Angry people

Anyone can be angry at times, but there are different ways of showing it. Anger is a chemical reaction, and is usually unexpected, sudden and over quickly. You can be angry at someone because of something they've done, and almost literally "explode"; this could be described as "hot" anger. But the other sort of anger is the "cold" variety, which happens when the chemical anger has subsided and has been replaced with thought patterns. Now the anger has moved to plotted revenge, which is much nastier and quite frightening. The difference is easily detected. Cold anger can take a long time to reveal itself and is controlled and deliberate. Hot anger is much easier to deal with than the cold variety.

Bullies

The behaviour bullies exhibit is usually unpleasant, offensive and unacceptable, but one of the worst things about them is their ability to make you feel as though you're a kid in the school playground.

Their major motivation is to make themselves feel "big" by making someone else feel "small". They are usually insecure or have been bullied themselves at some point or other. Displaying bullying behaviour is the only way they can gain any self-esteem themselves. They may be physically violent or threatening, or they may make personal verbal criticisms. If a bully picks on you at work, it is important that you talk to someone else (and someone trustworthy) about it. The only thing worse than being bullied is feeling isolated. The essential thing to remember when coping with bullies is that whatever they do or say, it is only *their* opinion of you, and this does not define who you really are as a person or what others think of you.

Hostile people

These people come in many shades, from cool and indifferent through unfriendly to downright insolent. Their influence can spread like an unwelcome virus throughout teams or entire departments. The atmosphere created by hostile people is unpleasant and needs to be purged at the earliest opportunity. Hostile people display negative characteristics such as muttering, snapping, ignoring or giving people the cold shoulder. They may have a grudge against someone from some past event; they may have something on their mind which colours their attitude to anything and anyone. They may have a chip on their shoulder, based on some form of inferiority complex. The best way of dealing with them is to find out why they need to exhibit such behaviour towards other people. They may not even realize that their behaviour is upsetting, in which case they need to be shown the consequences of their actions.

16   Insecure people

Maybe you know someone whom you regard as "fragile". You may have to be careful what you say to them, or watch the way you behave for fear of upsetting them. In the workplace, where people are busy and teams need to work well together, having one or two insecure people around can be quite a strain. It's like walking on eggshells, because you never know what they'll get upset about or when they're likely to fall apart. They are easily hurt; they may be worrying unduly about something. They can completely withdraw from communicating with other people if it is more than they can cope with. They magnify criticism and take things personally even if the remark was fairly mild. They are good at predicting future failure by thinking that "it is bound to go wrong if I'm involved". They need help and support, which should be offered sensitively.

Patronizing people

People who make others feel belittled or unimportant because they think they are better than everyone else are actually arrogant and insensitive. Some patronizing people are expert name-droppers. This is usually their way of showing off, displaying that they are superior to everyone because of their connections. When you see through their behaviour it usually becomes apparent that they are somewhat insecure and need this smoke-screen of self-importance.

However you are treated by a patronizing person (and it will feel a bit like being bullied), you should not take it personally. Many patronizing people behave this way either because they think they are superior as a result of having often been told so (maybe as a child), or because they need to feel they are above everyone else and are putting on an act. This behaviour becomes a habit with them, and the way they come across to you is not a personal thing. They treat everybody like this. You need to look beyond how they are behaving towards you, and see how they are actually communicating generally.

Unmotivated people

Do you recognize the uninterested, incurious, reluctant, slow, unwilling and clock-watching individuals in your organization? These are the unmotivated people who just can't or won't get involved or interested in their work. They may possibly be passionate about something outside the workplace, but inside it they are hard to stimulate into action.

For a start, they lack curiosity. If you were to say to them, "Don't you care about what you are doing?" they would probably say, "No, not really." Some people actually lack curiosity about their work, the purpose of their work, and the use to which their work will be put. It's possible that they've been told just to get on with it and leave the thinking to someone else. One way of stimulating some unmotivated people is to try to find out what they are interested in, even if it has no connection with their work. If you can get on to their wavelength, even a little bit, it may help to get through to them.

Coach's notes

However tough you find it to deal with other people, it will get easier the more you do it. If you don't try to tackle various situations, you will not learn. Overcoming shyness and fear is confidence building. Don't get too concerned about failing occasionally. Making mistakes is all about gaining the opportunity to learn. There are some people with whom building relationships is extremely difficult and complex, and it is going to take time. It is worth persevering, however, particularly if the person with whom you need to interact has an influence on your life – such as a superior at work.

Challenges are something everyone should accept as they progress. Meeting challenges will help you avoid being overtaken by other people, or prevented from improving yourself. Above all, it will enable you to keep control of certain events and situations.

Go for it! People can be difficult, and if you are prepared for this, you won't be taken by surprise when they behave badly at work. There are numerous types of people who are awkward and unreasonable, and they conduct themselves in varying ways – from mild to extreme. You will quickly learn what their negative behavioural traits are and what marks them out as a difficult person. Then you can identify which type of person is causing the problem by observing their conduct. Don't worry unduly about them "getting to you". Difficult people are the ones with the problem – it is rarely a personal attack on you, although it often comes across like it. And you are not the only person on the receiving end of their insults – this is their normal way of carrying on.

This chapter sets the scene regarding encounters at work. Sometimes the workplace is described as a jungle. Certainly there are lots of diverse characters you meet at work, but could they really be described as animals? Of course there will be some people whom you work with who do seem quite strange, and you may not instinctively know how to deal with them. But being successful at getting on with people doesn't mean you need to know everything about human behaviour. In this chapter, some basic rules for dealing with people effectively are set out.

CHAPTER 2

In the workplace

What happens at work

Does the office environment sometimes bring out the worst in people's characters? The answer is probably yes. Why should this be? Because people are often put under immense pressure at work to perform to their best ability. They are faced with tight deadlines, and sometimes they are required to produce pieces of work that are not purely a result of their own efforts. They may be – through no fault of their own – heavily reliant on others. If those on whom they depend let them down for whatever reason, there is a lot at stake. Instead of being reasonable and easygoing, they can undergo swift character changes. Failing to produce an expected result can have dire consequences for any organization. Not least there could be serious financial issues and career implications, and of course workplace relationships do suffer.

The workplace isn't, and never will be, a peaceful environment. With today's pressures, work can be a struggle, particularly when there are a number of competing personalities all vying to get things done their own way. When people behave badly, you need to spot them quickly and anticipate what damage they may inflict on you. Many

22 people carry out an avoidance strategy, coupled with a damage limitation exercise. Things have to be achieved, often in parallel, and sometimes the stress can be enormous.

Rookie Buster

When people behave badly, you need to spot them quickly and anticipate what damage they may inflict on you.

Acknowledging this fact is a start, but it needs to be taken further to make things easier. Confronting different character types with wide-ranging behaviour patterns on a daily basis can be physically exhausting. Maintaining the smooth running of a corporate environment is a complex process. If you are in a department where tempers get frayed, you will need to develop the right attitude. If you go to work each day anticipating a battle of wills with your colleagues, that is what you will probably get. Adopting a conciliatory approach instead may help you achieve a calmer atmosphere. Even when someone throws a tantrum, it is best to keep cool and your head down.

Colourful characters

Most individuals are under pressure from forceful personalities at some time or other. Coping with competition and dealing with challenging and diverse characters in the workplace does no one any harm. In fact in many cases it is a good thing – a form of positive stress. No one progresses far in an environment of apathy or complacency. Stress frequently stimulates performance, and it is a tactic many employers resort to, in order to work out who can cope and who can't. If you can't stretch or be flexible, you will break.

If, for example, you are entering a company at the first tier of the management structure, it is likely that the directors or partners in that company will pile the pressure on you as a young manager. You should be able to show them how successfully you deal with a workload that, at times, threatens to engulf you. If you are able to do this, it will give a clear indication of how far you are capable of rising. In addition to dealing with stress, it is important to show you can also cope with staffing issues. By maintaining a healthy atmosphere in your department, you will show how capable you are. Senior executives are always conscious of the importance of succession planning, and you would do well to bear this in mind when having to cope with difficult people.

Rookie Buster

By maintaining a healthy atmosphere in your department, you will show how capable you are.

Measuring pressure

Stress, however, isn't always a positive thing. If it reaches huge proportions it becomes compounded and negative. Your performance will be poor; you will find you are not able to deal with matters in a rational way. Lack of time, restricted resources, unrealistic deadlines and overwhelming details – all these things put pressure on you. Many people working in organizations often feel under immense pressure and unable to cope. It is not surprising that, as a result, their behaviour and tolerance levels are stretched to the limit.

It is easy in these circumstances to become a "difficult" person. You feel that the environment in which you are working has become hostile and unreasonable. You may react angrily to the situation and snap when provoked by others. If you feel this is happening to you, then you must take action, because otherwise your reputation could be adversely affected. Your experience, even if it is not huge, should tell you that being positive, keeping up to date with your work, extending and

24 improving your skills and thinking before acting makes you an effective person.

Rookie Buster

Many people working in organizations often feel under immense pressure and unable to cope.

But what happens when, somewhere along the line, someone else causes a glitch in the proceedings and a problem occurs? There may be all sorts of reasons for this, but it could well be the result of how someone else has behaved or reacted to a situation, and not necessarily the result of just one person's deliberate action. Suddenly a routine job, one that could perhaps have been easily completed between 9.00 and 5.00, allowing you to go home with a clear desk and conscience, becomes a battle of wills and a fight against time.

So why do "other people" conspire and undermine an individual's productivity and effectiveness? Opportunities get missed, but what's most upsetting is that in many cases people don't even realize that their behaviour has contributed to the problem. And before you put your hand up and say that whatever other people may do, you are certainly not guilty of causing havoc, wait – this may not be entirely true. There are few perfect people in the world. Your performance may be faultless in your own eyes, but this may not be the view held by your colleagues.

Rookie Buster

Your performance may be faultless in your own eyes, but this may not be the view held by your colleagues.

Attitude counts

It all comes back to attitude. If you can adapt your way of behaving by changing your attitude towards situations and colleagues, you can reduce the amount of chaos the divergent personalities cause in your workplace. Taking such action can avoid friction, and many negative situations will become positive ones. Remember that even where harmonious relationships exist, human beings will always have occasional trouble in dealing with each other.

Nowhere is this more prevalent than at work. Maybe you have a job in a place full of conscientious workers. These people are often severely underestimated, undervalued and underpaid, despite carrying out their duties competently. It is possible that there are a number of others with whom you work who are paid extremely generously for doing a lot less. What makes life problematic is the way they manage to do this, even profiting from other people's efforts at times. Should they receive promotion, this can bring out a lot of resentment and jealousy amongst co-workers. Tempers fray and rows flourish.

These other people's position, influence and salary far outweigh their capability. They are actually being dishonest – with themselves, their colleagues and the organization. They don't hesitate to take time out of the office for spurious and unimportant meetings. They are frequently negligent, delegating tasks to subordinates who are not qualified to do the work. If you've ever been blocked for promotion or constantly nagged to produce more work from people like them, it is hard not to feel bitter and frustrated by their Teflon-coated existence. In order to survive such situations, you need to work out the reasons why they occur, and arm yourself with a number of strategies to help you fight back. If you can adjust the balance in your favour, not just in relation to job satisfaction but also with regard to pay and conditions, you will

26 enhance your career development, and your relationships with co-workers will be more positive.

So what can you do to work around the difficult people and get what you want from your job? What are the secrets for making human relationships harmonious and effective, however perverse people seem to be? It is a huge advantage to be able to deal with tricky people and situations as and when they occur. Try to build amicable relationships and, where that is not possible, assert yourself so that you do not feel undervalued. This way you will develop your own strengths and personality at the same time.

Rookie Buster

Try to build amicable relationships and, where that is not possible, assert yourself so that you do not feel undervalued.

Waving not drowning

Companies cannot afford to stand still. Employees are constantly being encouraged to acquire new skills. You could be in a job where there is a merger or takeover, and redundancies are on the cards. You may get a new boss, be transferred to another department or be asked to do your job in a different way.

People who are taken unawares in such situations are at a grave disadvantage compared to those who are capable of embracing change. There are no longer jobs for life, and there is more flexibility in how people do their work. There is less need to conform in the strictest sense (such as by clocking in at 9.00 am, or wearing a uniform) so that you hold on to your job. Standing out from the crowd (in a proactive way) is the best way to get your next job, or promotion. Give yourself a head start by being able to react quickly and flexibly. Doing so in a positive, rather than a negative way, is the best method.

Rookie Buster

Standing out from the crowd (in a proactive way) is the best way to get your next job, or promotion.

The way you relate to other people in the workplace can impact negatively or positively on those who can influence your career. You may be able to act exactly as you want to at home, but at work your behaviour may affect your career progression. It is important to learn how to behave in order to exert maximum positive effect. Popularity is a bonus. If you have the ability to make other people feel good about themselves, you'll have a huge advantage over those who cannot. The most successful working relationships are built around mutual trust and respect.

Rookie Buster

The most successful working relationships are built around mutual trust and respect.

Respect for others can be as simple as saying good morning and goodbye to your colleagues when you arrive and leave. If you are sincere, show concern for their views and listen to what they say, and they will respond positively towards you. Don't forget to thank them when they communicate information. If you occasionally need to convey criticism, be particularly careful to ensure that it is offered in a constructive and positive way.

28 *Understanding the characters*

Most people you work with are reasonable, so dealing with them isn't a problem. But there are a few who have certain personality traits that it is useful to be able to recognize. If you encounter some of these traits, don't worry. Take appropriate action, and by doing so you also take control. This often results in discovering hidden depths, talents and strengths in yourself that you didn't previously realize you possessed. Here are some brief descriptions to help you recognize these problem traits.

Destructive

These people live to dominate, insult and wound others. They have an openly hostile attitude towards colleagues and can be sarcastic, uncooperative and arrogant. Their know-it-all attitude makes it extremely hard to get on with them. They won't hesitate to stab you in the back if it serves their purpose. Because you cannot trust them, you must tread carefully when you are dealing with them. They are usually self-appointed experts who, because of their huge egos, can never be wrong. They know everything and refuse to believe that anyone else has anything useful to say or contribute to the workplace. They include workplace bullies, patronizing and hostile people.

If you had to choose adjectives that described their character qualities, these could include:

- Bad-tempered.
- Unkind.
- Bossy.
- Predatory.
- Ferocious.
- Obstinate.

And if you were applying animal imagery to

such people, you might describe them as wild beasts, or safe only behind bars. They like being seen as mad, bad and dangerous to know.

Disgruntled

Everybody has encountered whiners, moaners and grouches. They display all negative qualities and are fully paid-up members of the "glass half-empty club". In their view, life shows them nothing but bad luck, and they are never happier than when they are miserable. They are expert nitpickers. The last thing they want is some cure-all for their woes. Solutions never feature on their horizon; they enjoy their problems far too much. They simply hate any colleagues coming along and showing enthusiasm for challenges. Their main reason for existing seems to be to throw a bucket of cold water over anyone with positive suggestions. Unfortunately their attitude is infectious and can spread like a bad dose of 'flu to other members of the workforce. These disgruntled characters include insecure and unmotivated people as well as blamers. Adjectives that describe them best include:

- Dissatisfied.
- Frustrated.
- Sulky.
- Complaining.
- Envious.

Colleagues refer to them as moody, crabby and carping. They are often bad tempered, and not all that friendly.

Dead-pan

These people are hard work. They don't have much courage, and hardly ever say anything about what they really think or feel. They would rather be invisible or remain hidden from view. They are colourless and negative. They'll do whatever it takes to avoid facing issues

30 head-on. Such people limit their communication to the occasional murmur. On a good day you might get a monosyllabic answer.

They are expert at concealing their feelings and frequently have a mysterious air about them. They talk in cryptic fashion, in hush-hush tones, and prefer to remain anonymous and behind the scenes. They veil their expressions, and their remarks and behaviour patterns resemble something clandestine, undercover, stifled and suppressed. It is not easy getting them to open up, so most people find it easier to give up and move away. Sometimes it is a case of "the lights are on but nobody's home" – in other words, there's really not all that much going on inside their heads. These people are also insecure, anxious, embarrassed and unfulfilled. The adjectives that could describe them include:

- Elusive.
- Solitary.
- Timid.
- Secretive.
- Remote.

Do these people ever come out of hiding? Their self-image is low or virtually non-existent. They are frequently overlooked and unnoticed, which adds to their discomfort.

Taking appropriate action

How many times have you found other people's disposition and behaviour affecting you? Isn't it hard work keeping up a sunny frame of mind while sitting next to a grumpy, scowling colleague? The ability to be impervious to other people's sighs, moans and groans shows that you are grounded and steady in your own personality. The last thing you need is to be undermined by the selfish behaviour of a co-worker.

Developing a thick skin helps, as does distancing yourself from colleagues who are boring, unpleasant or moody. Don't allow yourself to become a prey to these formidable people. If they detect a chink in your armour, they will home in on it like a missile and exploit your weaknesses. This makes upsetting you a whole lot easier for them.

Rookie Buster

The last thing anyone needs is to have their effectiveness undermined by the selfish behaviour of a co-worker.

If you are being affected (adversely) by other people's behaviour at work, you will need to develop skills to make you appear indestructible. These include verbal skills, negotiation and humour. (Chapter 5 examines these skills in detail.)

Verbal skills
Use words to defend yourself or support your point of view. If you have easy communication skills, you can use words as your ammunition against these troublesome characters.

Negotiation
By learning the art of compromise, or deal brokering, you can save yourself huge amounts of trouble. You should, with practice, be able to devise win–win strategies to get you out of the most awkward situations.

Humour
Humour is an essential aid to defusing tricky issues. By reducing the temperature of a heated argument, explosive feelings and tempers can be cooled. You may emerge from the argument unscathed.

32 *Office politics*

People means politics. Anyone who has worked for a large organization knows this. But even in smaller companies it is useful to be able to recognize the office politicians at work. No one can ignore this reality of life and survive for long, let alone prosper. Office politics have predominantly negative connotations – the phrase summons up images of backstabbing, Machiavellian plotting and watching over your (or someone else's) shoulder. When circumstances and people combine to conspire against you, the going gets really tough. There's nothing wrong with healthy competition between colleagues, of course, and most people would claim that it's a good thing; even a bit of friction isn't necessarily bad, either. It can act as a catalyst and stimulate creativity and output.

One of the simplest ways to combat the office politicians' efforts is to ignore their behaviour when you come into contact with it. Showing offence and being affronted puts you in victim mode straight away, which is an inferior position that you should not assume. Avoid being manipulated by them, otherwise you can't take control, let alone gain the upper hand. You don't stand a chance of coming out on top if you show signs of inferiority at the start. Keep cool and maintain your distance.

Rookie Buster

You don't stand a chance of coming out on top if you show signs of inferiority at the start.

Where ambitious office politicians are concerned, it is worth bearing in mind the following factors.

Intentions

However constructively they approach their jobs, people are not moti-vated solely by the desire to produce good work. They have their own agendas. Some of these include interaction and positioning with others. Personal ambitions can be strong and include:

- Getting the job done.
- Increasing personal job satisfaction.
- Organizing greater visibility for themselves.
- Impressing others.
- Securing greater rewards.
- Gaining power.
- Taking on more responsibility.
- Beating others in a race for promotion.

This list shows the areas of potential conflict, since a number of these points clearly involve competition. If one person gets more responsibility or is given greater authority while another is not, it will cause friction. These issues are all highly personal. To one person, being given more work involving, say, travelling abroad might be regarded as a perk. To another it would seem an ordeal, even though accepting the added responsibility would give either person an advantage.

Rookie Buster

If one person gets more responsibility or is given greater authority while another is not, it will cause friction.

Because of their personal agendas, people work to achieve what they want. This involves them pushing harder and harder to accom-plish their aims. They may even go as far as preventing or

34 handicapping someone else in their desire to succeed. This is where assertiveness changes to aggression, and brute force is used instead of more restrained behaviour. What they do may be secretively devised, subtly and even invisibly deployed. But it is still a ruthless action and has no other purpose than to obtain personal advantage at another individual's expense.

Additional factors may also be at work. Office politicians are inherently less concerned about others. They see things from their own viewpoint. Some have openly destructive streaks.

Appearances can be deceptive

Those who behave politically in the workplace may display deceptive personality traits. Things are not always what they appear. What is said may contain hidden messages and agendas. There are the usual known phrases to watch out for: "Trust me," "Let me be honest with you," "I'm on your side, here." Be alert to this, and read carefully between the lines as the communication continues. If you can determine people's motives, you will begin to interpret what they are really saying. It is wiser to be cautious than automatically thinking the best of them, or giving them the benefit of the doubt. Colleagues need to be assessed carefully. Are they potential friends, or enemies? Sometimes, confusingly, they may be one thing on one occasion and another at a later time.

Rookie Buster

If you can determine people's motives, you will begin to interpret what they are really saying.

Keeping a watchful eye 35

You should watch for, and read, any signs that could prove useful indicators. For example, notice:

- What is said.
- How it is said.
- Alliances and changes of allegiance.
- People's intentions and motivations.
- The behaviour of others.

What you should try to do is develop a way of working with your colleagues which embraces the political environment. No one can work in isolation; others can and will affect your progress. The only question you must keep asking yourself is, are they assisting or hindering it? Be careful when deciding who you take into your confidence. How much can you confide in them, and how soon? When should you ask for advice? How much should you publicize your success (or, conversely, hide anything that is less than successful)? Who should you know and who should know you? What do you want other people to think of you? All these questions and more are important. Each one requires that you make considered judgements. Above all, keep your ear to the ground and know what is going on.

The best way forward

The plan you adopt will depend to some extent on the style of those around you, and the culture of the organization you work in. All this makes the workplace sound like a minefield. It does pay to be watchful, but the way forward needs to include many others, not only the prime players. Don't exclude those who remain neutral in the overall game plan. They could potentially help in specific ways. People add to your knowledge and competence. A network of advisers, confidants and collaborators is always useful.

Take the people out of an organization, and nothing of significance would be left. They form the essential ingredient of any corporate

36 survival strategy. Having the right network cannot be left to chance. Your intentions should be decided early on. You should systematically work towards making and maintaining the necessary contacts to keep you informed about what is happening, especially if you're not able to work it out for yourself. If this sounds scheming, it is – but it is necessary. Without such a plan you will be defenceless against others. This is all part of organizational life.

Coach's notes

People, contacts, relationships and interactions all make working in an organization possible, interesting and fun. But the politics that go hand in hand with organizational working are full of potential risks. Worrying about who is on your side, who does not like you and who is seeking to score points will make life uncomfortable for you. By taking a realistic (but not pessimistic!) viewpoint about behaviour at work, and a proactive approach to understanding how to deal with it, you can do more than just survive in the workplace.

Go for it! Your goal is to find a way of being less of a target to those who like causing trouble. If you do not fear confrontation and refuse to permit certain individuals to intimidate you, you will succeed. Your way of working will enable you to operate effectively and achieve your own personal agenda. Being aware of what is going on and realizing that people do things for lots of different reasons does help. The right attitude is essential, and you should always focus on positive results.

Notes

This chapter goes into more detail about how to handle the destructive, disgruntled and unmotivated colleagues who were introduced in Chapter 2. It teaches you how to recognize them, what they are trying to achieve, and how to overcome their tactics and come out best in any potential situations of conflict.

CHAPTER 3

The main characters

Destructive colleagues

Have you worked with people who exhibit all sorts of unfriendly feelings towards their colleagues? Their behaviour and actions seem designed to make others fail, and they delight in others' misfortunes. They see winning as being the most important thing, usually at the expense of someone else. More often than not, destructive colleagues enjoy using other people to gain their own advantage. In the process, someone else is trampled underfoot. They are bullies and want the credit for everything.

The nature and range of their behaviour varies. Some of these unfriendly types may simply be a bit ruthless in the way they set out to achieve a small step up the chain of command (like acquiring a parking place when they are in short supply). Or, at the top end of the scale, they may regard a brutal character assassination attempt as their best route to promotion. This could mean that no one in the organization is safe, since they are prepared to go to any lengths to achieve their aim.

Destructive colleagues are easy to recognize. They are usually loud,

42   aggressive, hostile or arrogant. They will argue about everything, and have the tact and diplomacy of stampeding elephants. Other people are taken issue with at every opportunity. They can go as far as making you feel guilty just for getting to work and taking up space in the office. Being on the receiving end of such bossy and harsh treatment makes their victims feel intimidated. This escalates into an ever-growing cycle of unreasonable behaviour. Staff absences and changes increase dramatically in workplaces where destructive colleagues are a dominating presence.

Rookie Buster

Destructive colleagues are easy to recognize. They are usually loud, aggressive, hostile or arrogant.

At worst, these bullies do not confine themselves to their own team or department. Throughout an entire organization, destructive colleagues can be seen inflicting their offensive personalities on the unsuspecting, the innocent and the unprepared. For those who have the misfortune to work with them, it's always a relief when they are out of the office, on holiday or in meetings. They are often angry and rarely able to enjoy simple pleasures. Their idea of success and achievement is through antagonism, threats and other people's bad luck.

How to deal with destructive colleagues

One way to cope with destructive colleagues is to use guerrilla tactics and fight back. After all, they aren't dealing with you in a civilized manner, so why should you maintain a reasonable stance and put yourself at a disadvantage? By refusing to yield to their demands, you can begin to turn the tables on them and take control. It will come as a real surprise to them, because they're accustomed to their behaviour making people run away. Their intimidation methods usually work, so they will be thrown off balance by you standing up to them.

When faced with an impenetrable and unmoving opponent, destructive colleagues will be confused. Why isn't this person capitulating as usual? What is going on? It might be the first time they have ever met with resistance to their demands. By refusing to get upset, lie down or run, you will have faced the aggressor and turned the tables on them. They will probably behave in a more acceptable manner straight away, bluffing wildly that you have misunderstood them, and they never meant to be unreasonable. They certainly won't want to risk retaliation by your attacking them. They are unlikely to relish a taste of their own medicine.

Rookie Buster

When faced with an impenetrable and unmoving opponent, destructive colleagues will be confused.

One possible result of standing your ground and giving the impression of being ready to fight is that your destructive colleague may calm down. Although it is quite normal to adopt flight mode when an aggressive person explodes at you, doing so plays into their hands. The smart operator looks ready to kill, but doesn't fight and plays a waiting game. This forces the aggressor to think and, hopefully, reconsider their behaviour. Defusing the situation is essential if you are to take control and turn the tables on the predator. Destructive colleagues thrive on hostility. If you counter their offensive behaviour with a strong but non-aggressive response, they will have very little to fight about. This will disorientate them and they will run out of ammunition.

44   Subtle destructive colleagues

These people are possibly even worse. They enjoy wounding colleagues with cutting, vindictive remarks. Their abrasive comments can take the form of sarcasm and innuendo, as well as laughing directly at others or behind their backs. Behaving in this indirectly aggressive way can be even more hurtful than outright attack. They disguise their dislike of co-workers by creating false impressions, or showing insincere friendship. They are cowards and don't behave in an openly antagonistic way because of their fear of being attacked in return.

If confronted head on by those they've antagonized, the subtle destructives tend to protest that no harm was intended, despite the fact that a fair amount of damage has already been inflicted. Don't be misled by their behaviour: they know exactly what they are doing. Their aim is to wound deeply and cause maximum emotional damage. These people deserve no sympathy and are well aware of the injury their victim has sustained. They have to be stopped before wreaking more havoc in the workplace.

Rookie Buster

Demand an explanation as to what exactly is meant by a certain remark. This way you will force the aggressor into giving a response, which is exactly what they don't want.

Dealing with subtle destructives requires a different technique in retaliation. This is because a scathing remark can hurt far more than a bullying insult from a direct assailant. Demand an explanation as to what exactly is meant by a certain remark. This way you will force the aggressor into giving a response, which is exactly what they don't want. They are then faced with the possibility that you might launch a venomous attack in return. This usually makes them surrender immediately. They are craven, which is why they prefer these under-hand methods of attack. By standing your ground and insisting they justify their remarks, you will disturb them greatly. They will probably try desperately to wriggle out of giving a straight answer by bluster-ing, changing the subject or attempting to resort to humour.

If in doubt, do nothing

There is another form of response, which requires disengaging the emotions and behaving in an uncharacteristic way. The subtle destruc-tive is counting on having wounded your emotions and getting a reaction. The no-response reaction is not what they expect, and can deter this type of predator. Draw yourself up to your full height, take a deep breath, but give nothing away. The cooler and more unaffected you appear, the greater your chance of success. Hold your position: this buys you some time, and should be enough to help you regain control of your emo-tions. Your attacker is deprived of satisfac-tion, since their insults don't seem to have affected you at all. This is all extremely unnerv-ing to such an unpleasant adversary. If you show no outward sign of being wounded, they will be confused and not know what to do. You don't have to move or say anything. If you wait long enough, they will usually take themselves off, because they will be unable to work out what the next move is.

46 *Disgruntled colleagues*

These are the negative types who, although not the most difficult species on the planet, have the ability to infuriate patient and tolerant colleagues. They are full of blame, accusation, protestations of innocence, suggestions of injustice and pessimism. Nothing is ever really their fault. They flourish on being one of life's chief victims. They are the hard-done-by, the put-upon and the dissatisfied. While they may not antagonize or wound like the destructive colleagues described above, they can drive co-workers to distraction by their response to remarks, situations and requests for action. The net result is a draining away of positive energies from even the most upbeat and optimistic colleagues.

Disgruntled colleagues work on the premise that if something hasn't gone wrong yet, it soon will. Even if the sun is shining brightly outside, they will forecast a downpour by lunchtime. If you try to reassure them that the weather forecast said the opposite, they will not believe you and become quite irritated by your contradicting them. Managers or colleagues who are responsible for introducing any sort of change or improvement have a really uphill task dealing with them. Disgruntled colleagues declare it'll never work, or it has already been tried and has failed dismally. Their lives are a constant succession of insoluble problems, none of which are caused by them.

Rookie Buster

Disgruntled colleagues work on the premise that if something hasn't gone wrong yet, it soon will.

They see other people as continually conspiring to cause them inconvenience, injury and misery. If you enquire how they are, or even compliment them on the fact that they look well or have performed above the average, they won't accept it. Instead you may unleash a torrent of information about how they are close to death, or have just survived a dreadful crisis or some other near disaster. They also believe that no one cares, despite the fact that you've just asked how they are. The impression they like to give is that the whole department, if not the entire organization, is populated by heartless, selfish, blind characters who have never so much as glanced in their direction to observe their suffering. The implication is that managers, colleagues or staff should have noticed their plight sooner or known better. In the end you wish you'd ignored them and never spoken at all.

Even the most reasonable of colleagues will find defeatism hard to cope with. Every development, important or trivial, is supposedly the result of other people putting upon them. Luck might be regarded as a piece of positive fortune, but even when faced with an advantage, disgruntled colleagues have the ability to twist things around until they find a downside. These pessimistic personalities are never happier than when they are miserable. They use their gloom to attract attention.

Rookie Buster

Even the most reasonable of colleagues will find defeatism hard to cope with.

The main thing to remember is not to allow yourself to get caught up in their ploys by offering to help them or provide a solution. They are a bit like spiders spinning their webs. If you come too close or express sympathy, this is playing straight into their hands. Don't try to assist a determined complainer: they won't be in the least bit grateful. In fact, they will be even more upset because you are attempting to deny them their main reason for existing. They will straight away ferret around until they find another situation or person to have a moan about. They are so expert at this, it will take them only a matter of moments to achieve their aim. Draining in the extreme, it saps your

48 energy levels and brings you down to their level, which of course was their intention in the first place.

Complainers are forever victims. If you suggest that something they have done needs looking at, or improving, they will switch to martyr mode instantly. They will insist that it is only due to their best endeavours that the organization hasn't ground to a halt years ago. In an instant they will have turned the tables around, and you will be the guilty party. Not wishing to be at fault, you will be on the defensive and taking responsibility for the whole situation. If you pursue your original aim, which was to draw attention to aspects of their work which need improvement, you will risk provoking a scene – tears, sighs, sulks and the rest – which will have repercussions across the entire department.

These intensely negative attitudes can cause chaos in an otherwise buoyant group. Disgruntled colleagues should be regarded as highly contagious, because they can undermine the morale of the most optimistic of colleagues. But even though they drain your enthusiasm, energy and zest for life, there is no underlying objective with disgruntled colleagues. They are not Machiavellian types who have hidden agendas to wrest power from others to bestow on themselves. These people genuinely believe that they have no choice about the situation they are in. You can try to open up their cage of disappointment and hopelessness, in which they dwell quite happily, but they would rather that you joined them in their misery. Above all, you must protect yourself from their efforts – put up your defence shield and retreat to a safe distance. By remaining a bit aloof, or removing yourself from their sphere of influence, you should stay clear of trouble.

Rookie Buster

Disgruntled colleagues should be regarded as highly contagious, because they can undermine the morale of the most optimistic of colleagues.

Lending an ear

If you are able to listen, with patience, to the alleged grievances of disgruntled colleagues, you will show them that you are interested, and that you are trying to understand what their concerns are. You will need acute listening skills to be receptive to their problems. If you are successful, you may unleash a flow of complaints which are hard to interrupt. At some point you will have to interject in order to check that your understanding of the issues is correct.

Another successful tactic is gradually adopting a change of position. If you do this, you can gain an advantage over disgruntled colleagues. They will be so busy reciting their grievances that they may not notice the subtle change you have made. You could take a different slant of their argument and use their words to turn the tables on them. Another tactic is mirroring; this involves appearing to agree with disgruntled colleagues, who will not realize the deception. They will assume that tacit understanding means endorsing their views. By careful reasoning you can let them know you understand what they're saying, but it does not mean you agree with them. Avoid saying things like "You're right," or "I agree." If you do, they will respond with "I knew you'd agree I was right," which would in their view strengthen their position and probably unleash another torrent of complaints.

Another way of dealing with an expert moaner is to empathize and suggest a number of realistic options. Sympathy is what they want, but the more choices a disgruntled colleague is offered, the clearer you are making it that there is a possible solution to his problems. The crucial point to get across is that they have the responsibility to choose the most appropriate course of action. It is they who have ownership of the unsatisfactory situation, and a solution is within their grasp.

- Step 1. Show you understand the problem.
- Step 2. Stem the flow of complaints.
- Step 3. Offer two or more sensible choices of solution, then leave them to come up with their decision.

In order to get a result, you should try to establish that the dissatisfied person really wants to change things. Unless they can accept that they

50 have some responsibility for the situation they find unacceptable, and the consequences resulting from it, it will be impossible to move forward.

Rookie Buster

In order to get a result, you should try to establish that the dissatisfied person really wants to change things.

The plan is to get the disgruntled colleague to accept that he or she *chooses* the situation they are in. If they admit that, then they are able to take control. They cannot be both in control and a victim. If you've shown them that, they'll see that they can't have it both ways.

Offer a challenge

There is a way to resolve the situation of the negative person who continually depresses their colleagues: get them angry. This is a positive energy, which could help them to shrug off the weight of depression that lowers them. Provoke them; challenge them so that their anger is directed towards you. Insist that they are specific about what is irritating them, and help them to alter their view of events so that they take responsibility for their actions.

A complainer who is challenged by a series of direct questions to reveal exactly what he feels will either get angry so his viewpoint can be changed, or he will get so fed up with the process that he will refuse to continue. When dealing with chronic complainers, it can be pointless being gentle or diplomatic. Interrupt them forcibly, by raising your voice, or using gestures to stop them talking. You will need to connect with disgruntled colleagues by listening or challenging. Your aim is to help them make positive moves to accept responsibility for their situation. This takes time, objectivity and tenacity. but it is worth the effort, if you can do it.

Rookie Buster

When dealing with chronic complainers, it can be pointless being gentle or diplomatic.

Unmotivated colleagues

There are times when you urgently need a response from bosses, staff and colleagues. A lack of information under these circumstances can be quite frustrating. Colleagues who blank you and give no more than a grunt or a groan when you are hoping for some illuminating explanation are exasperating. But how do you tell if you're dealing with someone who doesn't talk, or who just won't talk? This is a bit difficult. Some people don't say much because they prefer to speak only when they have something interesting or significant to say. Others will retreat behind a wall of silence in order to express resentment or some other negative emotion. This can be extremely hard to deal with, because they can remain stubbornly unresponsive and resist all attempts from you to get them to open up.

Unmotivated colleagues can decide for a number of reasons not to communicate with a co-worker. It could be that they perceive you as a usurper of a position they covet, or that they disagree with you strongly over something you have said or done. Unless you can find out why this person is refusing to communicate, you could be in the dark for ages. The inscrutable never explain their motives or feelings, particularly to their victims. The solution is to be patient. If you are working alongside this person, you are probably seeing them on a regular basis. Try systematically moving towards them to show what sort of person you really are. The easier you make it for them to know you as a complete person, the less reason they have for rejecting you and giving you the silent treatment. Keep calm, treat them fairly and reasonably and they should find it impossible to continue with their attitude. In time they should behave normally with you.

Fear of giving information away is another reason why unmotivated colleagues behave as they do. Refusing to answer a question or responding only in monosyllables allows a person to avoid telling lies or sharing bad news. The silent treatment is a bit like invoking the right to silence in court. It can suggest there is much to hide. People suppress emotional crises by hiding behind a wall of silence, but if these feelings are repressed it can be extremely damaging to the person hiding the emotion. If you succeed in getting them to open up, you may be faced with a reaction that surprises you – tears, rage or bitterness. Whatever reaction you encounter, don't take it personally. It will not be you that is the cause of that individual's suffering. It may be embarrassing for the individual if their pent-up emotions are released at work. If possible, try to get to the cause of the problem and, if you think it is necessary, suggest they see their doctor, or take a few days' rest. You are not a therapist, merely a concerned colleague.

Rookie Buster

The easier you make it for them to know you as a complete person, the less reason they have for rejecting you and giving you the silent treatment.

Dealing with withdrawn characters is difficult. You need to help them to respond by asking a suitably worded open question. If you can, maintain eye contact even if there is a period of silence after you have asked the question. Your expression should remain encouraging, because the individual may need some time to formulate their response. If you think there is a relaxing of the facial muscles or some body language that indicates they are getting ready to speak, make sure your antennae are ready to pick up any communicative gestures. The silent colleague uses their silence as a form of power, because they know it is something most people are uncomfortable with. If you feel no progress is being made, simply repeat your enquiry and wait. This gentle interrogation technique usually works in time.

Rookie Buster

The silent colleague uses their silence as a form of power, because they know it is something most people are uncomfortable with.

While dealing with unmotivated and withdrawn colleagues, remember that they are very good detectives. They have spent so much time silently observing and listening to others, they can easily recognize when someone is asking them a question merely to have the opportunity to state their own opinions. They are over-sensitive and prefer to protect themselves with a defensive shield. The unmotivated will detect if you are sincere, but should you be the slightest bit false, they will not trust you. And because they are timid they sense danger far more accurately than their braver colleagues.

Coach's notes

You should now be fairly familiar with the way destructive, disgruntled and unmotivated colleagues present themselves. Some (like the destructive) require firm handling in order to limit the damage they can cause. The disgruntled need more studied approaches (listening or challenging), and the unmotivated require a good deal of patience. It is possible to achieve a change of behaviour with all of them, provided you are determined and resolute. Try some of these ways of handling difficult people when you next encounter them. They may need to be varied a little, because you can only achieve success by adapting your own behaviour until you get the outcome you want.

Go for it! If you are dealing with difficult people at work, don't take their behaviour as a personal attack. They could behave the way they do for many different reasons, none of which you are responsible for. You must protect yourself from their unreasonable attitudes by whatever means you can manage. Quite often you will find that it is not too difficult – the anticipation is far worse than the actual encounter. Be brave and try it for yourself.

Troubleshooting skills are what's required when you are dealing with difficult people. Chapters 2 and 3 contained information about some of the character types you could encounter. There was advice on how to deal with them if their behaviour was a direct challenge to you. This chapter offers solutions on how to get the best out of awkward situations where people are being un-cooperative. It deals with strategies. Without being aware of your own powers, having a plan and being able to deal with people, you won't get far. Knowing what you want to achieve is halfway to reaching your goal.

CHAPTER 4

Developing your strategies

Power

Do you regard yourself as a powerful person? Would you say that you succeed in most situations? Have you ever thought about it? Well, you are probably far better equipped to deal with difficult people than you realize. If you haven't already done so, you could usefully spend a few moments identifying what your strengths are, and where your talents lie. Should you be too modest to do this, ask someone whose opinion you respect to help you. If you are aware of your personal strengths, you are more likely to be able to use them to your advantage in awkward situations. People who know what they're good at and use this power appropriately are successful and in demand both inside and outside their organization.

Rookie Buster

If you are aware of your personal strengths, you are more likely to be able to use them to your advantage in awkward situations.

58 When required to do a bit of self-analysis, to work out your strengths and weaknesses, refer to your past appraisals. These should reveal your:

- Particular skills.
- Personality factors.
- Knowledge of your job/responsibilities/staff/organization.
- Connections and contacts.
- Profile and how you are perceived by others.
- Attitudes to your work and to dealing with people.

Self-analysis is not much use unless it leads to action. If you are conscious of what personal strengths you have, you will find it easier to work out how you probably come across to other individuals. You don't want to be another "difficult person" yourself. When you aren't sure how others perceive you, it is easy to upset them, however unintentional that may be.

Rookie Buster

Self-analysis is not much use unless it leads to action.

In every organization there are colleagues who can make your life easier or harder. They can be service providers, sources of information, seniors or juniors. They can sort things out when your computer fouls up, organize the sandwiches for your next meeting, or encourage you with your career plans. Whether they are above you, alongside you, or below you, most individuals you deal with will have issues at some time or another. Upsetting people by misuse of your power is a mistake. Unhappy, moody colleagues are time consuming and draining. They will make life difficult. Always use your power for the positive.

An individual's power can come from a number of sources. These could be:

- Your *experience* (previous jobs and positions you have held).
- Your *skill* (with figures or people or projects).
- Your *expertise* (ability to choose good staff or know which new products to promote).

Whatever your particular strengths, identify them and keep them in good repair. They should be readily employable, because you never know when you're going to need to use them. With in-house training usually available, and companies attaching great importance to knowledge sharing, it is sometimes difficult to hold on to your "edge" over others. The more training your colleagues receive, and the more you share your "special expertise" with the organization, the more your power source could diminish. It is always sensible to keep your skills and contacts as up to date as possible.

Rookie Buster

It is always sensible to keep your skills and contacts as up to date as possible.

Think about what abilities you have that are of value to your organization. What transferable skills do you possess which you used in a previous job and which could help you now? What or who do you know that could get you out of a jam and change a disaster to a triumph for yourself, colleagues and company?

Plans

It is always sensible to have a smart idea or two up your sleeve; you never know when you might need them. After recognizing and knowing how to exploit your power, the next most useful survival strategy is planning. Harnessing the power of preparation is an

60 essential skill. The surroundings in which people work can affect the way they think and feel. The type of work environment you prefer may be a bustling atmosphere, while others may perform better in a tranquil location. Some people require different situations for certain tasks. Analytical types perhaps prefer to work in a quiet area, and if there is no such space, they may become irritable and difficult.

Rookie Buster

The next most useful survival strategy is planning. Harnessing the power of preparation is an essential skill.

When you are faced with awkward situations and conflicting temperaments, in order to be able to get on with your tasks, the faster you can find a solution the better. Your objective should be to restore calm so that harmony will reign and people can continue working without further interruption. There are no golden rules or short cuts for solving problems involving people. That is why it always helps to have a plan. Being prepared is essential. Your plan may be simple, but because you're in a position to implement it at the appropriate time, it could avert disaster. Whether it's a minor dispute you're facing or a serious issue could impact adversely on the whole organization; being ready to take appropriate and rapid action is what is important.

Dealing with a difficult person or issue could mean that there is no time for reflection. Therefore any effort spent in advance will make things easier. Planning how to cope with a crisis will include:

- Knowing where to obtain any necessary information.
- Keeping your prepared plan of action ready to hand.
- Being able to activate your plan without delay.
- Having the confidence to proceed as you feel appropriate.

Take for example the scenario of a security alarm or fire alert. It's essential that everyone has been briefed beforehand as to where the emergency exits are, which staircases should be used in the building, who among staff is a qualified first-aider in case of injury, when to evacuate the building if ordered to do so and at what place to assemble outside. In the event, should other people be panicking, it will be a huge advantage if you remain calm in mid-crisis. Not only could it avert possible disaster, but everyone else will feel better because they will see that someone is prepared and able to take control. It could also give courage to others who are extremely frightened. They may behave surprisingly well under difficult circumstances, if they feel there is a responsible and trustworthy leader who they can follow.

Under such circumstances, you will show that you have power. People will see that you are prepared for the unexpected and can take action if necessary. This will raise morale amongst colleagues and create a positive image for you. Systematic preparation and planning is an excellent thing and will go a long way to restoring calm. When faced with a crisis, no one minds particularly who takes control as long as *someone* does. So do your homework, have a survival strategy to hand, and perhaps you'll never need to use it.

Rookie Buster

When faced with a crisis, no one minds particularly who takes control as long as *someone* does.

Getting results

In a situation requiring resolution, there are a number of processes that may need to be considered. Perhaps you're unfortunate enough to work with colleagues who are behaving particularly badly, causing disruption across a whole department because of continual arguments. If you were asked to deal with them, the first step could be:

- Arranging a meeting with the individual(s) concerned.
- Enquiring into the background of the dispute.

- Suggesting certain courses of action, such as training courses or conciliation.
- Locating specific information to enable the individuals to make a choice.
- Encouraging those involved to take responsibility for a solution.

Solution strategies always need to include:
- Who.
- What.
- When.
- Where.
- Why.
- How.

Part of the essential planning power pack is your reconnaissance and information gathering skill. When you are stepping into the treacherous waters of dispute resolution, you need to be certain you are familiar with the latest information, such as current organizational objectives, procedures and systems and the people involved. How can you begin to sort things out unless you know:
- Who is responsible for causing the trouble in the first place?
- What they actually did which triggered the issue?
- When the incident happened?
- Where it took place?
- Why the situation occurred (background history)?
- How it could best be resolved or avoided in future?

You may be looking at a sudden flare-up of temperament between some members of staff. Or it could be that one person has over some time been the victim of a bullying campaign by another colleague. If you do not have a plan for determining the influencing factors, you will not be able to come up with an appropriate way forward.

To continue with your planning as a trouble-shooting strategy, you will also need to be aware of:

- Lines of communication and reporting: who needs to know about this, are any meetings required, what other processes are involved?
- Controls: how should you monitor the progress of the dispute resolution?
- Policy: what rules and procedures apply and do you understand them?
- Records: what notes should be taken and who should do this?

To ensure you gain maximum power from your planning strategy, it is worth remembering the following factors that are involved:
1. Time.
2. Effort.
3. Thought.
4. Cooperation.
5. Outcome.

1. Time
Dealing with difficult people is something that takes time. It will affect your workload when you abandon what you are doing to sort out a problem involving others. Do be prepared for this, and build a buffer zone of time into your plan. Don't skimp when dealing with disputes involving people, because one thing is for sure – if you fail to put in enough time on the process, things will only get worse, or break down with cataclysmic results later on.

2. Effort
It is a challenge, albeit a worthwhile one if you achieve success. But as there are no magic formulae or quick fixes, you may underestimate the amount of effort that will be required to achieve a positive result. Plan for the energy you'll need to get that desirable win–win situation for all concerned. Without considering the challenge, and how much hard work will be needed by you and others, you may not succeed. If the parties involved are stubbornly determined to be difficult, you will require deep reserves of energy to achieve this.

3. Thought

Any successful outcome requires thought. A knee-jerk reaction or instant decision may not be for the best. Complex situations require consideration, research, analysis and thinking through. You don't want to make an already awkward situation worse by implementing a quick but intrinsically weak solution, just so you can say you've dealt with it in order to get it out of the way.

Rookie Buster

Any successful outcome requires thought. A knee-jerk reaction or instant decision may not be for the best.

4. Cooperation

You should be prepared to seek and take advice from others whenever you can. Don't assume you can manage things on your own. The saying that two heads are better than one is often true. Look to your own staff – colleagues as well as superiors – for their input. This could be crucial towards making the right decision.

5. Outcome

Mistakes can and will occur, despite the best laid plans. You can't win every battle, and you might have to lose a few to win the war. Don't be put off if you fail to achieve a solution; it may take more than one attempt. But if you learn from your failures, the experience will prove an invaluable lesson and you're not likely to repeat the error.

When making plans, remember that the best ones tend to be circular. The planning process is more powerful if it is continual, as this promotes on-going success. For example:

- The *attitude* you have towards your strategy leads on to …
- The *actions* you need to take, which are followed by …
- The *focus* you bring to bear on …
- The *key issues* of the problem, which involve …
- The *relationships* you cultivate with those involved, which directly affect …
- The *habits* you create for yourself in dealing with others, which relate to …
- The *attitude* you have – and so on and so on.

Enough said about planning. You should move on (swiftly!) to the third strategy.

People

You will encounter people of all sorts in the workplace. Some you will get on with, some you will not; some will help you, inform you or teach you. Some will infuriate you; some you will work with, getting things done that would not happen without their help. But, male or female, young or old, senior or junior – most, if not all, will at some time or other irritate you. Because interactions in business are intrinsic, these problems cannot be avoided. You simply have to find a way to work round them that minimizes the disruptive effect they can have on you and your work. Here is an example that is useful for everyone.

Harnessing people power

Maybe your expertise lies with building teams? If it does, well done. You are ahead of the game already. If this isn't one of your strengths, consider what an unfair advantage it could give you when dealing with challenging personalities.

Creating a productive, efficient environment depends on working in harmony with others. Teamwork skills are immensely useful and a great source of power. The combined power a successful team wields is far greater than if they operate as individuals. The power you can generate if you are capable of harnessing other people's energy, skills and expertise is a vital asset. If you can equip yourself with this ability, almost anything is achievable. Good teamwork means group motivation and creativity. Use it wisely, and you will find great things can be done and success is the most likely outcome.

Rookie Buster

Good teamwork means group motivation and creativity. Use it wisely, and you will find great things can be done and success is the most likely outcome.

Good teamwork involves working closely with colleagues, communicating effectively and being able to persuade and negotiate with others. Although some people are lucky enough to be born with such characteristics, many others have to work hard to perfect these skills. Some people think that everyone has to be the same to make the team a success. Making the most of each individual's natural strengths and personality is an important aspect of good teamwork. If you possess the ability to recognize other people's strengths, you will be able to work out a winning team structure. This is a hugely powerful asset for any department or organization.

Perhaps you already possess some of the qualities that make an expert team builder. Maybe you find it easy to make the effort to be sociable and build good relationships with others. Perhaps you are a good listener, and take note of others' ideas and try to build on these. Are you able to respect colleagues' opinions, even if you don't always agree with them? You need to be detached and place the groups' objectives in front of your own agenda. This is particularly difficult for those with big egos. Are you good at encouraging and motivating other

people? Do you readily offer assistance and support when it is needed, 67
and know when and how to ask others for help in return? Are you able
to compromise, negotiate and be persuasive when necessary?

If you can do all or some of these things, you will find there are lots of
powerful advantages to be gained. You will almost certainly have your
capabilities recognized and be appreciated by others in the organization. Being open minded, you will acquire knowledge from others who
have different abilities and perceptions to your own. The power of team
building means you are capable of establishing productive working
relationships and also effective at dealing with conflict. The important
thing to remember, as part of a team, is that everyone has a responsibility to help create a climate in which everyone works harmoniously.

Rookie Buster

The important thing to remember, as part of a team, is
that everyone has a responsibility to help create a climate
in which everyone works harmoniously.

This is most effectively done by:

- *Showing respect to members of the team* – valuing them for what
  they are and their individual qualities. Respect doesn't mean
  having the same values and interests. It is possible to respect
  people you don't like.
- *Building rapport with them* – if you ask the rest of the team what
  they want or what's important to them, they will realize you have
  their best interests in mind. They will then be more prepared to
  cooperate with you.
- *Being sincere and understanding* – communicating clearly and
  sensitively with the others, but not allowing your personal energy
  to squash the rest of the team's goals and ambitions.

The best way to avoid conflicts occurring within the team is to build strong, healthy, open relationships with them from the outset. In teams where honesty is present, disagreements can be aired and, hopefully, more easily resolved. Without trust among team members, they will be fearful of expressing opinions openly. This usually results in a huge amount of energy being used to solve the conflict, resulting in loss of time and creativity.

Rookie Buster

The best way to avoid conflicts occurring within the team is to build strong, healthy, open relationships with them from the outset.

Some suggestions for dealing positively with conflict among teams:
- **Independently expressing a viewpoint**, even if it is a dissenting voice. An effective team will be able to accept an alternative approach should it be appropriate.
- **Avoiding insults to preserve self-respect.** Put-downs are not a way forward, and will do more to obstruct progress than a restrained approach which is impersonal and objective.
- **Lowering the temperature.** To reduce tension within the group, perhaps introduce a word of encouragement, a perceptive remark or humorous comment.
- **Accepting other team players as they are.** It is unlikely that you will change other people's attitudes and behaviour. When trying to resolve divergent viewpoints, it is easier to compromise than change an opinion.
- **Showing confidence in the team.** If you have a flexible approach, you will be a helpful and supportive member of the group. A committed team understands the importance of the enterprise. Success depends on understanding the objective and making a combined effort.

To summarize, when using the power of people in relation to harmonious teams, it is worth keeping in mind the main functions. First
of all, make sure you have:

- Definite team objectives – this includes identifying the task and
  its limits. Check that appropriate targets are set, and involve every
  one of the team players. Agree each individual member's targets
  and responsibilities.

With regard to the planning aspect of team relationships,
establish:

- What the *priorities* are, and how decisions are going to be made.
  Sort out a team structure and how tasks are to be delegated.
  Assess the skills of each person, and if necessary arrange skills
  training if there are some glaring gaps.
- *Communicating* with the group appropriately is essential; without
  this nothing will be achieved. Make sure there is a clear brief, and
  check everyone understands. Consult with the team, and ask
  them to reflect on the situation and give feedback. Remember, you
  may be required to listen or advise, but always remain positive
  and enthusiastic.

Teams require:

- *Support*, from each other as well as from the leader. Progress
  should be monitored and you should check that standards are
  being maintained. Watch out for any signs of lack of coordination.
  Should you be concerned, put in immediate effort to reconcile any
  conflicts that arise. Recognize that difficulties can and will occur,
  encourage team players to pull together, and offer counsel to those
  members who need it.

Any team action requires:

- *Evaluation*. Set up a review plan, adjust the goals if necessary and
  summarize what actions have been taken and why. Be unstinting
  with praise. Everyone benefits from being thanked and
  appreciated. Should failures occur, make sure the lessons learned
  are positive and constructive.

You should allow all team members the opportunity of:

- *Appraisal* of their performance. Offer guidance and training should they wish it, and prepare for the future by evaluating their joint and individual achievements. Recognize that your best chance of survival depends on the team and the positive and harmonious interaction of task, team maintenance and individual needs.

Coach's notes

If you want to be successful at dealing with difficult people, you need to know what your own strengths are. This is your personal power pack. In order to deal effectively with awkward situations, you need to have a plan or two to hand. Finally, if you want to reduce conflict, develop the skills of a successful team builder. Should your colleagues work well together, there is less opportunity for them to cause conflict and strife. Power, planning and people are three essential parts of the trouble-shooting package. They will help you to survive and thrive in the workplace.

Go for it! Remember, your power can come from a number of sources. These could be your experience (previous jobs and positions you have held); your skill (with figures or people or projects); or your expertise (ability to choose good staff, or knowing which new products to promote). Whatever your particular strengths, identify them and keep them in good repair. They should be readily employable, because you never know when you're going to need to use them.

Notes

The previous chapters have described relationships in the workplace, some of the characters you can meet and a few strategies for survival. This chapter describes some basic rules for communicating when faced with complex situations and awkward people. Considering how easy it is to misunderstand what people mean, it is surprising that there are not more battles in the workplace. People don't like confusion, particularly when they are being asked to do something or respond to a particular situation. If they don't understand what is going on, what is being said or why things are happening, they can easily get upset. If you learn clear and concise communication skills, you will be in a strong position to help defuse conflict at work.

CHAPTER 5

Communication techniques

Getting the message

When colleagues misunderstand others, they make incorrect assumptions and judgements. This affects their attitude to work, and causes problems across the team or department. You will be in a strong position if you can instantly switch on, tune in, pick up signals, and understand codes of behaviour. At work you are often surrounded by less than clear communication, whether spoken or written. Consider the amount of jargon, business-speak and gobbledegook that predominates in the commercial world. It is churned out with ever-increasing frequency. It comes as no surprise that people can't cope and throw tantrums because they are confused or unsure about what is expected of them.

Rookie Buster

You will be in a strong position if you can instantly switch on, tune in, pick up signals, and understand codes of behaviour.

Three areas of communication are described here: verbal, negotiation and humour. All of these, used correctly, can help defuse misunderstandings with your co-workers. What follows is a brief explanation of each, and how they can help when dealing with difficult people.

Verbal communication

Verbal communication in the workplace, if it is not going to land you in trouble, needs to be done well. It requires a lot of concentration, because it is all too easy to end up with both feet in your mouth. It is far easier to misunderstand someone than to get their meaning, particularly if they are not a skilled communicator. The skills and techniques you need for dealing successfully with customers, suppliers, colleagues, managers, supervisors and staff can be learned, but require effort and practice to ensure satisfactory results. The most important of these when dealing with challenging co-workers is the art of verbal communication. Whether you are involved in a formal meeting, a presentation, an informal gathering, or a one-to-one exchange, you need to get your message over to your listeners clearly, calmly and without misunderstanding.

Rookie Buster

It is far easier to misunderstand someone than to get their meaning, particularly if they are not a skilled communicator.

Preparation, planning and thinking ahead play a vital part in this process. If you have a clear idea why the conversation is taking place and you have worked out your objective, you will have a greater chance of communicating effectively. In this context you'll need to be as verbally persuasive as possible. Why? Because you are trying to get someone to move their position or viewpoint. You are attempting to:

- Defuse a confrontation.
- Get acceptance that a solution is needed.
- Achieve some reconciliation.

By remaining calm and keeping your remarks unemotional, you will be likely to attain the result you want. When communicating verbally with demanding people, a gentle tone will get you further than a hectoring manner. Expert communicators construct and use an argument to encourage their colleagues to respond positively to their message. In most situations, the people with whom you are communicating have a choice about how to respond. They can either accept or reject the message they are given.

Being persuasive

The more verbally persuasive you can be, the more likely you are to be successful. A compelling element will be necessary should your objective be, for instance, to encourage some colleagues to take on a task they've already indicated quite strongly that they do not wish to do. Perhaps you have the unenviable task of obtaining the agreement of some employees to work overtime at a weekend to get an urgent order delivered on time.

Rookie Buster

The more verbally persuasive you can be, the more likely you are to be successful.

The art of successful verbal communication when dealing with dispute resolution is to approach the process with the two viewpoints firmly in mind: your position, and the position of the opposition. You

78 know what your objective is, but what do you think your co-workers want? Depending on how generally difficult your colleagues are, or how stubborn or entrenched their position is, your best starting point is to work out what they'll need to hear to make them calm down. Assessing their level of objection, anger or distress will be crucial in choosing your words and manner of delivery.

So that your verbal communication can be successful, there are three points that you should bear in mind to help you to assess the situation accurately:

- How people feel.
- What they want.
- How they go about making a decision to agree to act.

Colleagues will recognize fairly quickly if you are trying to persuade them to do something they don't want to do. Depending on their mood and how troublesome they are, or intend to be, their instinctive reaction may be to dig their heels in. They may declare adamantly they're not being pushed into doing anything, whatever you might offer them. Your verbal communication skills face a challenge here. If you can focus on what the possible benefits are to them, they may begin to appreciate your motives. Why are you trying to persuade them to respond positively? Because they will also gain from the situation, if they agree. Perhaps a variety of negative feelings have arisen. Your colleagues' reactions could well form a barrier to further verbal exchanges. If they are strongly opposed to what you are suggesting, it may be impossible to progress the dialogue, because they are unwilling to allow it to proceed.

Emotional intelligence

Understanding other people's feelings is not easy, but it is essential to have some ability to predict their thoughts. When dealing with sensitive issues

where emotions are involved, it is easy for rows to escalate. Try to keep your feelings in check and remain detached, concentrating on what is factual. The less emotionally charged the exchange, the more likely it is that a compromise will be reached.

Rookie Buster

The less emotionally charged the exchange, the more likely it is that a compromise will be reached.

The outcome these colleagues desire will relate to their:

- Situation.
- Opinions.
- Experiences.
- Mood.

They may have deeply held views which go back a long way, built up by feelings of resentment and injustice. Conversely, their feelings may be much more topical, such as a swift reaction to a current problem or recently issued directive.

Rookie Buster

Understanding and responding to people's desires is an important part of being verbally persuasive.

Sometimes it is possible to anticipate what people will want, which will help you decide on the most appropriate verbal process. If there has been a slow build-up to a troublesome issue which you are now attempting to deal with, you will need a well-reasoned argument. On

80 the other hand, it may be just a matter of playing it by ear and seeing what comes out of discussion. Understanding and responding to people's desires is an important part of being verbally persuasive. Above all, make sure your communication method reflects a willingness to listen to their side of the subject.

Making it work

So how do you make this process work? In general, both sides want the same thing – a win. The best outcome is a resolution of the dispute that is acceptable to all concerned. The differing viewpoints need to be balanced if agreement is to be reached. You are the persuader, here, so you probably feel your view is right. After all, it is the other side's unreasonable behaviour that is the cause of the problem.

Before any progress can be made, the other side will have to adjust their actions and reasoning. Don't worry about persuading them to change their views dramatically or abandon the course of action they have embarked on. You should simply try to convince them that a move slightly towards your view and away from their extreme stance would be a great step forward. What you are hoping to achieve is for both sides to approach the middle ground.

Rookie Buster

What you are hoping to achieve is for both sides to approach the middle ground.

Whatever kind of compromise you are trying to secure, the persuasive process should assist the other side to make a decision without risking too much humiliation. This is the whole purpose of verbal communication in dispute resolution. You are not trying to impose something (such as sanctions or blame) on the other side. What you

are trying to do is to encourage them to revise their opinion or pos- 81
ition towards a more reasonable one. And if they do concede, this
positive movement by them should be acknowledged immediately.
The intention here is to help people to help themselves, as well as to
bring the temperature down to normal.

Movement means progress

Verbal communication that persuades people away from extreme situations is not something that can be directed at them. At best you can
try to engage them in a dialogue that will bring them towards the
desired position with an open mind.

People can be persuaded only by:
- Considering their options.
- Looking at the advantages and disadvantages.
- Selecting what seems to be the best course of action.

Defusing difficulties amongst warring colleagues may not be possible in every case. But, as an able communicator, you should be able to
bring into focus some key points of conflict. Two especially important
factors here are:
- Projection.
- Empathy.

These act together. If you project too much, you could give the
impression of being dictatorial and aggressive, which is not going to
help because you'll be mirroring your colleagues' approach. Too little
empathy and you will seem remote, insensitive and uncaring. Sufficient empathy softens what might otherwise be seen as too powerful
an approach.

Going back to the situation where you need to persuade staff to do
something they're strongly opposed to doing, how are you going to
achieve a satisfactory outcome? Provided your approach is flexible and
recognizes and exploits your colleagues' self-interest, you should have
some success.

Rookie Buster

Sufficient empathy softens what might otherwise be seen as too powerful an approach.

The content and delivery of verbal communication needs to be geared to:
- The overall objectives of the situation.
- The level of complexity involved in the dispute.
- The mood of your colleagues.
- The likely effect on them.
- The outcome required.
- The context in which the message is delivered.

And your communication's success depends on its being:
- Understandable.
- Attractive.
- Credible.

To be understandable in dispute resolution, you must be clear and concise. With angry or disappointed people, the greater the clarity and precision of your message, the stronger it will be. If you can make what you say immediately and easily understood, the important points will be conveyed to your colleagues unambiguously. You should try to make the proposed resolution attractive too. If you can persuade them that agreement is desirable, they may accept your view and consent. But this involves focusing on benefits rather than sanctions.

Rookie Buster

To be understandable in dispute resolution, you must be clear and concise.

Effecting closure

Adding credibility to your argument by offering a plausible set of reasons will make your case sound. Credibility can be simply quoting past experience, involving the support of others who are influential, or mentioning some guarantees that will result if agreement is reached. Practical techniques that can facilitate persuasive verbal communication include gaining the attention of the other parties, soliciting feedback, and anticipating and handling objections. Once you have explained your case, and all objections and queries have been dealt with, it is important to effect closure.

Rookie Buster

Once you have explained your case, and all objections and queries have been dealt with, it is important to effect closure.

Reaching a satisfactory agreement in a dispute requires action to be taken as a result of the exchanges. If there is still some element of indecision, and action is not forthcoming, you have not closed the deal. You will need to follow up swiftly on why the parties have not responded. In a worst-case scenario, you may have to repeat the verbal persuasion process all over again.

Verbal communication when dealing with difficult people needs to be conciliatory and convincing. You should construct your case to

84 encourage the other side to respond positively to your proposal, or act in a certain way. If you can convey the message that there are advantages to agreement you are more likely to succeed. Persuasive communication is an interactive process; you are helping people to make a decision. If you get it right, the decision they make is likely to be the course of action you are suggesting. Depending on how successful you are at recognizing and exploiting the other side's fundamental self-interest, you should be able to organize some movement towards middle ground.

Rookie Buster

Verbal communication when dealing with difficult people needs to be conciliatory and convincing.

Negotiation techniques

Dealing with difficult people in the workplace is emotionally demanding. Taking responsibility for conflict resolution and negotiation, and forming and sustaining healthy working relationships can use up huge amounts of energy and time. To deal with these situations successfully it helps to be aware of your own emotions and those of others. If you can project yourself into the opposing side's position, you will find this awareness an asset in expressing yourself appropriately. You will also be able to anticipate the needs of the people you are dealing with. The previous communication technique covered the necessary skill of verbal persuasion. Being a good communicator is a key element in conflict resolution. Before you can contemplate

sensitive negotiations, you will need to be able to interact well with people whose opinions you do not share.

85

The talent of negotiation

This talent is best acquired by practice. Here are a few suggestions to get you started. "Heads I win, tails you lose" is not a particularly good way of approaching the negotiating table, at least not if you want a successful outcome. Negotiation isn't about you winning and everyone else losing. Good negotiation is about a win–win situation. Both sides should feel that they've got something they wanted, or at least are in a better position than when the process started.

Rookie Buster

Good negotiation is about a win–win situation.

Planning your negotiation strategy is the first step. Think of all the potential objections your colleagues may raise. How can you convince them of the advantages of agreeing to what you have in mind? Try the following:

1. Describe the situation.
2. Express how you feel.
3. Specify what you want.
4. Clarify the consequences.

There are no guarantees that this will work, but if it doesn't, try to work out what went wrong and find a clear way forward. You could either adapt your requests, highlighting further benefits to your plan, or offer another more suitable compromise. Unsuccessful negotiation is where one of the parties feels that they have conceded too much, given way when they didn't want to, and been unduly pressured into making a decision that doesn't solve the problem. This is the "lose–win" situation. The other side may think they've won, and feel good about the outcome. This is the "win–lose" scenario. But that cannot be considered a success either.

Winners and losers

If a real negotiation takes place, there should not be a winner and a loser. If there is, the usual result is that the loser will not trust the winner, and won't want to repeat the experience. There's no point in winning battles if ultimately you lose the war. Negotiation is an interactive and balanced process. It involves:

- The initial stance – the starting point, or first offer, which may be something unreasonable.
- The point of balance – the stage at which a deal can be reached, even though it may not be the "best" solution.
- The win–win negotiation – in which both parties are satisfied and feel comfortable with the result.

The best outcome is something that is agreeable to both parties. Where there is a strong adversarial element, each party will be driving the hardest possible bargain. Each side will be trading something (terms, conditions, price), and give and take is necessary. It becomes a sort of ritual, as the parties move towards each other and apart again as the process continues.

Rookie Buster

There's no point in winning battles if ultimately you lose the war.

The key factors in negotiation techniques are:

- Information.
- Time.
- Power.

Information

Both parties in a negotiation want to know as much as possible about the other. Clear understanding on both sides allows more accurate and relevant reasons to be put forward in the bargaining process.

Time

This can add pressure to the negotiations, depending on how urgently a resolution is needed. When a deadline is imposed, it removes or reduces the negotiator's control of the situation. This adds stress to an already complicated issue, but deadlines are often themselves negotiable.

Power

Many factors add weight (or power) to the ability to negotiate. The two most usual ones are the power of *precedent* (what has happened in the past) and the power of *legitimacy* (whether the terms being negotiated are part of company policy or legitimate in terms of factual evidence).

Seeking common ground

Negotiation is a constructive process, requiring proposals to be made and discussed. It may at times be adversarial, but in order to achieve long-term resolutions, the overall aim should be a mutually agreeable outcome. Above all, it is about seeking common ground, which is the essence of good dispute resolution. The parties involved will have objectives, and in order to progress to a satisfactory outcome an agenda should be followed. This will involve:

- Asking questions and listening to the responses.
- Offering information.
- Honestly stating a point of view.

88
- Bridging a gulf between parties.
- Treating the other side with respect.

In essence, the negotiation process is an exchange that involves the presentation of proposals and counter-proposals. First you will need to work out your objectives – a clear idea of what results you want. Next you need to consider the variables – those factors that can be varied and arranged in different ways to produce potential deals. In addition, successful negotiation (like dispute resolution) involves using a number of basic techniques, listed here. If you can learn these, they will be immensely helpful when you come to tackle more complex situations. They are:
- Silence – a pause may make a point or provoke a comment.
- Attention to detail – never lose track of progress.
- Be reasonable – keep the tone of voice neutral.
- Use perception – to read between the lines and identify signals.
- Concentrate – keep thinking and maintain control.
- Variables – concessions that either side can make.
- Timing – deadlines in negotiations are usually flexible.

Negotiating involves the process of making a deal and agreeing terms. It is an interactive and balanced process, and although it may seem adversarial, the overall aim is a mutually agreeable outcome.

Humour

Shared laughter can release tension in the most awkward of situations. If you can harness the power of amused detachment when trying to get to grips with complex issues, it will help take the drama out of a crisis. Having a sense of humour in times of difficulty makes a serious issue less traumatic. Problems are only as awful as you allow them to be, and humour challenges accepted ideas. Some people have a readily accessible sense of humour, while others do not. Not everyone finds the same things funny, but there are some people who find nothing amusing. This is usually due to a conscious effort to take everything seriously.

You might think being serious at all times makes you seem more important, but having a sense of humour is an asset and a powerful skill when you are involved in resolving disputes. If you don't take things too seriously, and can laugh at situations, you are able to look outside yourself and be objective. You will also find it easier to deal with complex issues. You won't instantly identify yourself with them, and will instead be able to maintain a certain detachment between the issues and yourself.

Rookie Buster

Having a sense of humour in times of difficulty makes a serious issue less traumatic.

Aim for a smile

Humour usually provokes a smile rather than outright laughter. It is a liberating force, because the painful illusion under which you have been labouring is suddenly dispersed by a burst of amusement. Your sense of humour is an important resource in your dealing with difficult people. It can be used to take the drama out of a sensitive situation, and it is a great neutralizer of other people's anger. You can't laugh and be angry at the same time!

Rookie Buster

You can't laugh and be angry at the same time!

There are many occasions when humour can be a great asset – for example:

- When you have to deliver a difficult message.
- If you want to say no without causing offence.
- When a problem is becoming obsessive, you can re-think.
- As a release of tension after hard work – a safety valve.
- During a conflict when there is no sign of a solution.
- To regain people's attention if they have switched off.
- To build bridges or overcome barriers of age, education, and so on.

Having a sense of the ridiculous can be a huge advantage in difficult workplace relationships. Humour makes people laugh, or at least smile. When was the last time you laughed out loud? Was it at something you saw, something you read, or something you heard? You can laugh alone, but in order to amuse others you have to experience something funny yourself. Laughing is contagious. To use your sense of fun to lighten difficult situations, you have to be able to laugh readily and regularly on your own.

If you want to have a readily available sense of humour, don't get too depressed by and bogged down in all the bad news. Reading every newspaper and listening to all the round-the-clock news channels on TV to get the latest reports on the world's conflicts, financial crises, famines, epidemics and disasters won't cheer you up. Most news is negative and exaggerated. That's what sells newspapers. If you read a paper every day, you will get a daily dose of negative news. If you limit it to, say, twice a week, the amount of depressing information you absorb will be less.

Perhaps you've noticed that however upbeat you are, if you sit next to, or get into conversation with, a person who is gloomy or miserable, your good mood tends to evaporate. Keep away from bad news and depressed people. In times of stress or danger, there's often an opportunity for humour. It revives the spirits in the shadow of adversity. Making people smile usually involves an element of exaggeration or dramatization, to make something more outrageous by increasing its size and effect, or miniaturizing, thereby reducing the fact.

Rookie Buster

Keep away from bad news and depressed people.

Using humour in confrontational situations buys you some time. If you can get the other side to smile or laugh, you have for the moment neutralized the tension in the proceedings, and you will have a moment or two to re-organize your thoughts. Laughter prevents people from losing face, and eases the strain in exchanges. If you have to deliver bad news and you can combine it with a comic remark or an amusing statement, it will avoid causing offence and will neutralize a possibly aggressive response. A skilful use of humour can also help you to defuse uncontrolled anger and avoid the possibility of it escalating into violence. Observe someone who uses humour well: their body language, expression and face light up and it is difficult for others to maintain a hostile attitude.

Coach's notes

When dealing with difficult people, it is important to be a good communicator. When you are talking to people, whether delivering information or solving a conflict, your meaning must be easily understood. If you are in the process of delicate negotiations, it is essential. How can you achieve progress if the other side is unclear about where either party stands or what is on offer on the negotiating table? A further skill which can be usefully employed is humour, which is often helpful in reducing tension and aggressive situations.

Go for it! Becoming an effective communicator will be a great asset to you throughout your career. You will be able to put your viewpoint across easily and without ambiguity. You will be able to develop negotiating skills, which are always in great demand. The ability to empathize and listen to other people's arguments is advantageous. If you can persuade people to move from their position because of the way you put your case, you will be an asset to your organization. Using humour appropriately is also a skill which comes in useful from time to time.

The previous chapter described some important skills in dealing with difficult people and awkward situations. Two of these were good verbal communication skills and the ability to negotiate. Sometimes, however, when things don't go according to plan some extra ammunition may be useful. If you can restore calm and order when the going gets rough, your skills as an arbitrator will bring you to the notice of those in high places. You will be invaluable to your organization. It will also result in your co-workers being more cooperative and in having a pleasant environment in which to work. This chapter explains what else you can do.

CHAPTER 6

Tough tactics for tough situations

What is unreasonable behaviour?

Difficult people are bad news anywhere, not only at work. Did you know that "unreasonable behaviour" is the most common ground for divorce under English law? It's an often-used term in a number of different contexts, but how do you define "unreasonable"? There's no definitive answer. Something that is completely unacceptable to one person may seem almost normal to another. You can probably recall being in a situation where the atmosphere seemed to you to be embarrassing or awful, and all you wanted to do was to get as far away from it as possible – although maybe others who were there did not seem uncomfortable at all with what was happening.

Any difficult situation between warring colleagues, however, is likely to affect you and quite possibly the whole department. If you can cultivate the ability to create calm in the face of a storm, it is going to reflect well on you. Those who excel at dispute resolution are equipped with an awesome talent, and one that is always going to be in demand within any work environment.

96   When dealing with difficult colleagues you are likely to encounter people who are:

- Angry.
- Impatient.
- Rude.
- Stressed.
- Depressed.
- Frustrated.

Remember, these people may be completely unaware of how their behaviour affects others. Difficult people don't necessarily want to be difficult. Perhaps they are problematic because they aren't doing a good job, and don't know what to do about it. Could they have been promoted beyond their ability? Perhaps they have technical skills but are hopeless at working with other people in a team. Being a good worker doesn't necessarily mean you will automatically know how to get on well with others. Someone who has recently been promoted may be afraid of losing face, or even of losing their position. This could result in them being overly controlling, or conversely trying so hard not to dominate that they fail to communicate at all. They could be far too demanding and critical, or fearing conflict they may avoid dealing with problems and just ignore them.

 **Rookie Buster**

Difficult people don't necessarily want to be difficult.

If you are going to intervene to any purpose when people are behaving threateningly, you need to have:

- Personal integrity.
- The respect of others.
- The trust of others.

Without these, you won't be on a level playing field. Personal integrity is important. If you develop honesty from the start, your professional relationships with colleagues, staff and superiors will be positive and strong. You may be asked to help devise a solution because people will know that you have a principled and honourable approach. To be successful in brokering a deal or resolving an impasse, having good relationships with people in the workplace is a great asset.

Developing these qualities will mean your relationships with co-workers are healthy, in good times as well as bad. These relationships will be valuable, not just in the short term, but over a long time. You will not be looking at the solution of a problem as a quick win for yourself or the company: your desire for a satisfactory outcome will be for the benefit of all parties, not just of the organization as a whole. This holistic approach is the best possible outcome.

People with high standards of personal integrity are invaluable to any organization. To be one yourself, you should:

- Be direct in getting what you want.
- Treat people with respect.
- Avoid being antagonistic or aggressive yourself – even if you are on the receiving end of such treatment.

Rookie Buster

People with high standards of personal integrity are invaluable to any organization.

If you can manage this, you will not alienate people and will instead gain their goodwill. But not doing so could mean that people won't allow you to try to negotiate with them either now or in the future.

Here are a number of ways to deal with difficult characters.

1. Assess the situation

Remember that unless the protagonists are bullies, their behaviour could well be due to ignorance or misunderstanding. If the situation has occurred because of limited or incorrect information, it will be a lot easier to deal with. You can ignore their anger while you take steps to rectify the mistake.

2. Try to be supportive

If at all possible, try to support your colleagues. You want to come across as a healer, not an exterminator. Your colleagues will see your attempt to support them as an unselfish action, and the result may be that their behaviour improves.

3. Stand up for yourself

Don't tolerate being shouted at or verbally abused. If people are behaving badly, remember that they do not have the right to treat colleagues in such a way. Tell them that their attitude towards and treatment of others is unreasonable, but do so in an unemotional way. Being assertive is often the best way to halt unacceptable behaviour. It takes courage to speak out, but in many cases surprise is most effective.

4. Record the problem

It's very important to keep written notes about any dispute resolution process. Keep a record of incidents as and when they occur, and where possible make sure you have witnesses. Your organization may have a zero tolerance policy should the situation escalate to something as serious as harassment or bullying. If you have to go to the HR department for help, they will need evidence of the problem.

5. Getting the measure of the troublemakers

There are a number of motivators when dealing with troublesome and awkward colleagues. Managing the moods and actions of people you work with depends largely on your ability to understand them. Facial expressions and body language are great pointers as to how people are likely to react. Watch carefully for any signs they exhibit. One of the most obvious types is an angry person.

Dealing with an angry person

When dealing with an angry person, there are six steps towards achieving a peaceful solution: listen, repeat, accept responsibility, inform, ask and agree.

1. Listen

Should one of your colleagues become angry about something, don't respond by losing your temper too. The first step in dealing with an irate person is to find out the reason why he or she is upset. Is it your fault or the company's? Is it his fault? The next thing you need to do is to listen. It's important to let the person vent his anger, even if it is straight in your face. You must keep cool, and show that you are sympathetic to his situation. He will (eventually) calm down. Show concern by saying things like "How frustrating for you," or "I can see how infuriating that must be."

2. Repeat

Once he's expressed his feelings and realized that you are listening and understand his predicament, he will become (probably visibly) less upset. Anger is usually a short-term emotion. The key to allowing someone to explode is realizing that his fury will accumulate and fester until it is released. Someone who is allowed a one-sided shouting match will be more cooperative later on. Listening and acknowledging the emotion he is experiencing will help him to calm down. You will have convinced him that he has your attention. Repeat back to him the essence of his complaint, to make sure you have understood him clearly. It could be that you're the unfortunate recipient of some stored-up anger from other things which have nothing to do with the issue you're trying to sort out, but don't take it personally. Next, try to take back control of the situation once you've heard the person out. Tell him you will help solve the predicament. Focus on the issue and the possible solutions, not the emotions. If the person becomes abusive or potentially violent, explain that you want to sort out the problem if he will tell you (calmly) what he wants. If appropriate, ask a superior to help you.

3. Accept responsibility

Before taking any steps, make sure you understand the criticism, objection, request or need. Consider the possibility of human error. Perhaps he has been misinformed or he may not have all the facts. If there has been a mistake, it is best to admit the fault. Be open and say how sorry you are.

4. Inform

Explain how the mistake happened, if you know. This usually has the effect of taking the angry person entirely by surprise, because it is so rare for anyone to admit they've messed up and to take responsibility for working out a solution.

5. Ask

You need to establish what sort of solution will appease him. Offer alternative suggestions, not just one. But so long as you offer to put things right in a reasonable way, he is likely to end up feeling much better. Not only have you resolved the problem, you've also been honest with him.

6. Agree

Make sure your colleague realizes that you are taking personal responsibility for sorting out the problem until it is resolved satisfactorily. Identify the time scale. If the issue cannot be rectified immediately, tell him how long it is likely to take – even if you fear this may involve a further outburst of indignation.

Other difficult people

Here are a few more difficult characters you might recognize.

The capricious

These types love you today, but hate you tomorrow. Their mood swings are probably due to being under pressure. If you can get them to explain what is causing them to stress out, you'll be able to help them

102 achieve their targets or have more realistic goals. Quite often a problem shared is a problem halved. They will feel better having talked the issue through with someone sympathetic, and this may help them to exhibit more balanced behaviour.

The late tasker

This character is no trouble at all until there's a deadline looming and then, suddenly, the late tasker hits the panic button and the whole department is in turmoil. You may find yourself being asked to work all night to help avert disaster. Why should you pitch in to finish a presentation which ought to have been completed days ago? It's not really your problem, and you know that. You are also well aware of who is the cause. However, in the interests of the company and your colleagues, you decide to give the late tasker your assistance this time. The way forward is to insist that it cannot happen again. Ask for clear communication about any future deadlines and be up-front with ideas on where the late tasker can get help with time management. He needs advice on how to work more effectively, so as not to rely on others to dig him out of trouble.

The illusionist

Illusionists simply don't know what they are supposed to be doing. They don't cause too much trouble until they are challenged. But when asked to provide information on a particular issue, or produce results of a project that they were given responsibility for, be prepared for things to fall apart. If the problem is serious and has consequences for the organization, make sure you've kept records of any communications you have had with this person. Your own work on any joint activity with them should be separately documented and you will need others to confirm that you worked independently to progress aspects of the project where you had input.

Big brother tactics

What if the atmosphere in the department is impossible because of checks and balances? There is always someone who is compiling a survey or league table or performance indicator, or some target or other. This can inflict immense pressure on some workers. They feel "big brother" is watching their every move. When this sort of surveillance affects the performance of key people, it can have a knock-on effect throughout the team, department or company. Other people's self-esteem and output can be undermined.

There is a fine line between identifying workers' personality types to ensure smooth departmental operation, and constantly looking over the shoulders of employees. Plenty of companies claim to trust their staff to get on well with each other and their work, but then spend ages monitoring and measuring their behaviour and activity. Don't fall into the trap of looking for trouble everywhere – obsession with how everyone is interacting can be counter-productive. Keep things in perspective and take an objective and balanced view. Human capital is a valuable asset to any organization, which is difficult to express in hard financial terms.

Rookie Buster

Keep things in perspective and take an objective and balanced view.

When dealing with challenging situations among colleagues, don't rely exclusively on hard facts. Try to look beneath the surface and make an assessment of their emotions. Successful troubleshooters learn to trust their instincts. There is weighty evidence that intuition is a finely tuned and highly evolved decision-making process. Emotions positively influence our judgements and often are a better guide than the intellectual processes of the brain. When resolving disputes and differences between warring colleagues, use your emotional intelligence. The rational decision can sometimes be wrong.

Persistence pays

You may find that getting a resolution takes time, but don't be put off if you think your progress is slow. Human relationships can't be fixed by just pressing a switch. When bringing people together, remember these key points:

- Make sure everyone has the relevant facts.
- Combine verbal and written communication methods if necessary.
- Take control of a situation where someone has "lost it".
- Hold your nerve and keep going.

Keeping cool will gain you time. If you can reduce the temperature, you will save people from being upset. In addition you will help the "difficult person" by showing them a way of changing their confrontational attitude to a more positive one. To bring about a resolution, you'll need to be a committed mediator. You may have to arbitrate until a solution is found. Most situations are redeemable, though, if there is enough flexibility to bring about a compromise.

Rookie Buster

To bring about a resolution, you'll need to be a committed mediator.

You must be prepared to dig deep enough to reach the root of the problem. This could be something which was buried a long way back, such as a deeply held view. Good intervention with difficult people requires tact, patience and determination. But it also requires insight

– knowing when to press forward and when to hold back. Show neither fear, nor impatience. Simply hang on in there until some movement is made.

Straight talking may be required as well as persistence, but as long as the person you are dealing with really does, in some way or other, want a result or reconciliation, you will find a solution.

Be determined to get a result

Don't hesitate – troubleshooters get to the point as quickly as possible. Be logical and honest. But make sure you have some leverage – that is, some sort of power (emotional intelligence for instance) – otherwise you will face a really uphill task in getting a result. If you get frustrated and hampered by normal tactics, you may need to break the rules. There's nothing to be gained by being stuck in a rut. If no progress is being made, what have you got to lose? You know how irritating "blockers" or "jobsworths" are. They appear at every level in an organization, but the problem is that the higher up the food chain they are, the more power they wield and the bigger the blockage they can cause.

Rookie Buster

If you get frustrated and hampered by normal tactics, you may need to break the rules. There's nothing to be gained by being stuck in a rut.

If you are troubleshooting and faced with an impasse, reflect on what could have gone wrong:

- Have you been you mediating as well as you could?
- Have you been dealing with the right person (that is, the main protagonist)?
- Have you been oversimplifying the situation?

106   •   How direct have you been?

If you don't achieve a successful outcome, get on with the debriefing process and learn from your mistakes. Appraise your actions honestly, and take steps to improve your approach next time. Your instincts at picking up other people's signals, such as facial expressions and body language, will be more acute as a result. This is a big advantage. And don't underestimate the power of silence; it can make the other party reveal what they really think. The moment you turn a "no" situation into a "yes", you will feel a great sense of achievement. You may consider tackling an even greater problem next time without worrying about failure. You're on your way to becoming a great troubleshooter!

Coach's notes

The best way to become an expert at solving disputes is to use the six-step plan, suitably adapted, for the anger management scenario ("Dealing with an angry person") described above.

1. Listen to the person's objection.
2. Repeat back to him to ensure there is no misunderstanding of his complaint or problem.
3. Accept responsibility for sorting out the problem (this is not the same thing as admitting the problem is your fault).
4. Inform him what steps you are going to take to rectify the situation, and make sure he understands this.
5. Ask him questions relevant to the issue, such as what solution would be most acceptable (and if you can offer several options, so much the better).
6. Agree the next step towards resolving the issue. This may take one or two attempts, but keep going.

108

Go for it! You will need to be tough and tenacious when dealing with more complex situations, particularly where people may have very determined views or feel extremely aggrieved. If you take things a stage at a time, you will make progress. It won't be easy, but each time you attempt to resolve a situation it will get less traumatic. Be brave, be persistent and in the end you will be successful.

Notes

When faced with awkward situations caused by colleagues, problem-solving skills are what's needed. People who are good at this are quick thinking, have a good memory and are flexible when faced with a challenge. There are a number of techniques available to help, all of which become easier with practice. This chapter gives you some guidance on the basic steps of problem solving and identifies a number of situations which can occur in the workplace.

CHAPTER 7

Problem solving

Personality issues

Problems between staff often start with small snags; if these are allowed to grow, they can cause headaches for everyone concerned. Small differences of opinion may start the process, but the conflict then escalates as people become defensive, aggressive and sometimes malicious. By the time it is obvious that something must be sorted out, positions have become entrenched. It has become as much a battle of wills as a tangible problem.

Discussion is often the best route out. It may help to see different people separately at first, in order to hear their view uninterrupted by argument. Then perhaps both, or all, parties need to sit down together and discuss the matter. Such a session calls for a strong mediator – for example to ensure that only one person talks at a time, and that there are no interruptions. Listening, note-taking and recapping regularly helps to make sure that everyone is moving forward together. By keeping your manner calm and businesslike you should be able to maintain order and ensure that the resolution is a rational one.

Rookie Buster

Listening, note-taking and recapping regularly helps to make sure that everyone is moving forward together.

It is vital to take the heat out of situations. This may involve curtailing an argument and reconvening the group when tempers have cooled. Many people are embarrassed by conflict, whether their own or other people's. It is often uncomfortable being on the sidelines during another person's argument, and even more so if you are invited to take sides. People should always be encouraged to take a rational viewpoint. If you are the elected peacemaker you must strive for this.

Some people agree to disagree in certain respects. This is acceptable as long as any misunderstandings have been ironed out. The need to work amicably should override what may be seen as unimportant or petty bickering. People need to be drawn to a point where they can work together. As a last resort, it may be necessary to remove a person who simply refuses to exist peacefully and constructively with others. This could be done by reorganizing staff, or – if someone's behaviour warrants it – by dismissal. Clear rules of expected corporate behaviour usually ensure that matters do not reach such a difficult stage, however.

First steps

If you're trying to sort out a problem caused by a breakdown in working relationships, get as much information as you can as early as possible. The ability to retrieve information accurately and quickly gives anyone an advantage when faced with a challenge. There may be colleagues at your workplace who have been around for a while and know a whole lot more about it than you do. If so, it is worth checking up with them to get the background before attempting to unravel a tricky dispute.

Rookie Buster

If you're trying to sort out a problem caused by a breakdown in working relationships, get as much information as you can as early as possible.

To help you in dealing with difficult people who have caused unpleasant situations, your memory skills are essential. These involve:

- Recognition.
- Analysis.
- Identification.
- Alternatives and options.
- Consequences of actions.

If you assume the role of peacemaker in conflict situations, you are probably facing a deadlock between members of your team (or from elsewhere in the organization). Other people are relying on you to provide a solution. Before you start, here are some good points to bear in mind:

- Get to the root of the problem.
- Keep calm and in control at all times.
- Deal with things impartially.
- Lay down clear rules of behaviour.
- Deal with matters through discussion, not argument.

The processes and approaches involved then require that you:

- Give the problem-solving process adequate time.
- Listen, and be seen by others to be listening.
- Investigate and deal with matters in context.
- Aim to build bridges that will lead people away from conflict.
- Remain non-judgemental.

114   Some problems can be solved more effectively in a group. The question to ask yourself straight away is whether there are suitable and relevant people available to work together to find a solution. This involves combining the experiences and skills of others. Should you decide on group action, consider whether the problem is defined in many different ways. If it is, information from a number of sources may be available. Is the problem very specialized, or does it have implications for several other people? How many solutions could there be? If it is a complex problem with a number of differing factors, the solution will need to be agreed by others before it can be effective.

Rookie Buster

The question to ask yourself straight away is whether there are suitable and relevant people available to work together to find a solution.

Finding the cause

Start by finding out the cause of the problem amongst your colleagues, because you must know what sort of dilemma you're up against. There are plenty, but here are a few that commonly occur among workers.

The deviant

A special new project is under way. Everyone in the department (or organization) has been given specific instructions as to what is expected of them. Things should be running smoothly and without hitches. Suddenly you're confronted with a problem that you didn't realize existed. What's the cause? A member of staff has deviated from the planned course of action and has taken off in a completely different direction. This has thrown the whole project and team off course.

Everyone in the department is blaming someone else, and chaos is about to erupt. You need to rectify the situation quickly. To do that, you have to get to the root of the problem.

What are the possible causes?

- The task was not monitored sufficiently.
- Members of staff have not been adequately supervised.
- A piece of work has been delegated to the wrong person.
- The communication at the planning stage lacked clarity.

The improver

The system you are using at work is not brilliant, but it is satisfactory. A bright spark in the department suggests that he can sort it out. He promises to get results for the company that are better, faster and cheaper. Impressed, the boss gives him responsibility for delivering change. In the event, these improvements don't work, vital information is lost and all the standard processes are jeopardized. The rest of the staff round on the innovator and a huge falling-out ensues.

Find out what went wrong. Was it:

- Inappropriate delegation?
- Handing out responsibility without sufficient checks?
- Obtaining insufficient detail about the action to be taken?
- Appointing an individual rather than the group to deliver results?

116   The shirker

It has been obvious for some time that the IT system in your organization is not adequate to cope with the amount of work generated by the various departments. This matter has been raised a number of times. On each occasion the manager responsible has prevaricated. This is pointed out to a line manager, but not acted upon in time. A failing IT system could seriously affect the company's ability to operate in both the long and the short term. Action must be taken, otherwise problems will occur sooner or later. When the accident does happen (computer files are lost because of an inadequate IT back-up system, for example), everyone screams for help. You become a firefighter in this situation, and prompt damage limitation is crucial.

What do you do?

- Identify exactly what has happened and how.
- Shut down the system and stop the processes to avoid further trouble.
- Plan to conduct a full analysis after everything is made safe.
- Estimate the cost of the damage.
- Select the best and quickest route back to operational status.
- Set up a contingency plan to avoid a repetition.

The dreamer

A colleague has been nominated to design, build and implement a novel process. He is a creative thinker, and does not fully understand the problems that surround those who work in various departments in the organization. His work is impressive, and the directors are enthusiastic about his "blue sky" approach. They give the go-ahead without considering whether it will really meet the needs of the company. Colleagues are up in arms because they have not been consulted, and are threatening to walk out if the new system is implemented.

How do you avoid a mutiny?

- Have a detailed discussion with the "dreamer".
- Find out how his ideas will actually translate into reality.

- Call all colleagues to a brainstorming session.
- Identify any ball-park benefits from the new system.
- List colleagues' concerns and listen to their suggestions.
- Report your findings to your superiors.

As seen above, the problem-solving process involves a number of stages. Once you understand the component actions, you can use them in almost every difficult situation.

The problem-solving stages

1. Problem identification

The first issue is finding the problem which needs to be solved. The situation that has arisen is not the problem itself. Some problems may be obvious; others need to be teased out of those involved. Maybe there is only one small problem, but could it grow into something much bigger? What is frustrating people and making them irritable? Being able to categorize a problem is essential. With a bit of practice you will be able to look at how problems arise and recognize areas of potential conflict. The earlier you identify a troublesome issue, the more easily and quickly you can remedy it.

Rookie Buster

Being able to categorize a problem is essential.

Become aware of the areas in which problems may arise. You can do this by specific methods of detection such as: monitoring performance against certain targets; observing colleagues to pick up on behaviour that might reflect an underlying problem; listening to people if they wish to raise concerns; and conducting regular reviews that

118   compare current and past achievements in order to ensure early detection of any falling standards.

Would you, for example, be able to identify whether you were looking at a maintenance problem or an achievement problem?

You will need to be able to distinguish between these two, because each requires different analysis, and the remedies are not the same.

The *maintenance problem* needs a record to be kept of all previous standards, which reflects all aspects of deviation from the norm. This information should be analysed to identify possible causes. Each ground for concern should be tested against known facts to identify the root of the problem.

An *achievement problem* requires an accurate identification of all the objectives that have been agreed. Make a list of the characteristics of the current and desired situations. Work out what obstacles are preventing the goals being reached. Determine whether this is a process-related issue or a people problem.

Once you have identified the problem, you will need to set up a system to resolve it. Whatever you call this process – whether "problem analysis", "problem solving" or "project management" – it is applicable in most situations. Get as much information regarding the problem as you can from those involved. This is often termed the "group solution". You should try to find out from colleagues what their best ideas are and what they are trying to achieve.

Then you must ask what has already been tried and what stages were involved. Find out from those concerned what the benefits will be of solving the problem. Without tangible benefits, the problem may not be worth the time and effort involved in achieving a solution.

Rookie Buster

Find out from those concerned what the benefits will be of solving the problem.

2. Problem definition 119

What was the event or action that triggered the problem? You should aim to know what the problem is, and have a fairly detailed picture of the actions and events leading up to it. The next step is to identify exactly what issue it is that you want to solve, change or improve. At what level do you want to effect a solution? If drastic action needs to be taken, do you have the necessary resources (either financial or human)? It is sometimes difficult to distinguish between the root cause of a problem and the symptoms. Complex problems are often the result of many smaller ones combining. Maybe the problem is so large it will need to be divided up into sections in order to solve it.

Not all problems are acute, and some may not be important enough to merit the resources required to solve them. Even if they do require a solution, it may be sensible to wait rather than act hastily. If you run through the following checks, you should be able to decide whether immediate action is imperative or whether it would be better to wait.

- Would the problem, if left, be likely to solve itself?
- Is the problem, or the obstacle causing the deadlock, diminishing?
- Are the issues likely to be costly to the organization?
- Will these escalate if ignored?
- What likely knock-on effects are there?
- Are any of the problems time sensitive?

If the answer to the first two questions is no, and the answer to the last four is yes, then you should act immediately.

3. Selection and evaluation

When you identify a problem, it is not always appropriate to conduct a full analysis at the start. A brainstorming session with your colleagues or staff is however essential (see the group solution mentioned above). This should be done as swiftly as possible. There may be some benefits from certain swift actions, or on the other hand there may be no benefits from changing anything instantly. The purpose of the

120   brainstorming session is to see whether a "best solution" is obvious. If it isn't, you will need to come up with a system to select a best idea and develop it into a solution. Involve others either when you have a formal obligation to consult them or if you require additional information to help you in your evaluation.

Ideas need to be evaluated on the basis of what benefit they will give. If no benefit will be derived from them, you must be firm and move on. Start to generate other ideas and assess them. Essentially this is a qualitative analysis based on cost and benefit. Achievement problems could have a number of possible solutions, whereas maintenance problems have only a few options. Identifying the required information is often based on the problem definition. To do this well you need to know (1) what information is needed and why, (2) where or from whom it can be obtained, and (3) how reliable it is likely to be.

Rookie Buster

Ideas need to be evaluated on the basis of what benefit they will give.

Ideal solutions are rare. Some criteria to bear in mind when deciding if a solution is appropriate are:

- How great are the benefits which are likely to be derived?
- How effectively does the solution deal with the obstacle?
- How readily will it be accepted by other people?

There are a number of factors that could count against a possible solution – for example, limited resources, minimal acceptable results, and the disadvantages accompanying the solution being difficult to tolerate.

If you have a number of solutions available, you should be able to eliminate some less viable ones by applying the reasoning above. It will

then be necessary to evaluate the ones that remain and estimate how
close they come to being the "ideal" solution.

4. Planning

Planning techniques are common to large and small projects or problems. When planning a solution you need to keep three important things in mind: what are the needs of the business; are the staff capable of the performance required of them; how much will it cost the organization to implement? You will also have to plan for its implementation: who, what, when, where, why and how to make it work.

Who
Communicate with the people involved in order to gather the information and record it systematically. You will need to check the accuracy of the information received.

What
What action is going to be taken to remedy the problem? This requires a structure and a simple recording of events, which will be helpful in evaluating its effectiveness.

When
When is it going to be implemented? Is it going to be a quick decision? If it is, why? If the action is to be delayed, those involved in the process need to know the purpose behind the timing.

Where
Where is the change going to take place? Does the action relate to the whole organization, or is it limited to a small department or group of individuals? Is it taking place on site, off site, nationally, globally?

Why
Why is it being done? The answer should include the obstacles or the causes of the problem being dealt with. Also the constraints of the

122 situation, the characteristics of the "ideal" solution and what benefits will result.

How

How is the action going to be made to work? Be open about the risks involved and how acceptable the plan is likely to be to those involved or affected. These explanations can only be answered fully after you have decided on the possible solution.

When planning your action, have a schedule to help manage the process, and review your strategy to ensure its accuracy and appropriateness. Have the necessary resources (people or finances) readily available and select, brief and train those involved to make sure they have all the required qualities and skills to assist you.

5. Selling the idea

It is crucial to get the support of all those involved – whether that is the board of directors, the finance department or whoever is required to authorize the change. It is equally important to make sure that staff and colleagues agree with the changes, and are in favour of them being implemented. If you do not meet these two conditions, you are not in a position to move forward.

To encourage people to accept the solution, and to gain their commitment to it, you need to identify areas of possible opposition. How could the solution adversely affect those involved? What actions will be required of them when it is implemented? What they can expect from the solution, and what benefits they will derive from it, will indicate their likely degree of support or opposition. Ask them what they feel about the problem and what your solution offers. The answers to these questions will reflect their relationship with you, their perception of you and how much they respect and trust you.

You may find it helpful to make a presentation to persuade or convince people of the advantages of your proposed solution. This presentation could set out a number of reasons to counter opposition, as well as encouraging others to get involved, justifying your proposed use of

resources and showing your willingness to listen to objections and
make concessions.

Rookie Buster

To encourage people to accept the solution, and to gain their commitment to it, you need to identify areas of possible opposition.

6. Implementation and maintenance of the system

Before you set a start date, make sure you have in place the necessary structure to supervise the action and monitor its effects. Explain the solution to everyone involved, and get everyone to agree to it. Keep it on track by promptly countering unexpected delays, snags and obstacles. Your system should notify you if targets and performances are not met, and it should be one that all staff can use. Issues and problems should be reported as they arise. Make sure you are in control and that you review and analyse results. Compare the outcome of the action with the anticipated results. Are there any discrepancies; if so are they positive or negative? Take further action if necessary, either to correct a shortfall or to maintain current results.

Coach's notes

Any challenging situation can be turned into a problem-solving opportunity. You don't need to wait for a crisis to be imminent before jumping into the fray. You can approach almost any everyday situation to see whether there is something that could be done better. What is essential is that you bring about an improvement. You will make progress and get the support of others if they see you really are trying to change something for the better.

Forget about going for a quick fix – problem-solving that involves colleagues takes time. Sorting out problems with people's behaviour is not like flicking a switch – it takes effort, and requires a lot of thought. The most obvious solution may not be the best. With careful research, analysis and thinking you will get it right. Sometimes you will need help from others: not every problem can be solved on your own. This may mean bringing people forward to assist in meetings and mediation sessions, or seeking advice from those who can point you in the right direction from their own experiences. Finally, problem-solving may not always go right. Don't worry; failure is a great opportunity to learn. This is how many people gain their skill and expertise.

Go for it! Almost every problem at work concerning difficult colleagues can be handled by implementing what you have learned in this chapter. You should, with luck and practice, get reasonable results. When trying to solve problems in the workplace, you need to be able to look at a situation objectively, see where people are not happy – and then be prepared to do something about it.

One of the keys to successful people management is being able to work out in advance how others may react to certain situations. This means knowing them and understanding their situation. When faced with difficult people, your ideas may run counter to theirs – they want to make trouble; you want to avoid it. Opposing views may be strongly held. If neither party is willing to yield an inch, be prepared for confrontation. You will need to gain the upper hand if you are to overcome the problem. This chapter gives some suggestions when dealing with complicated characters and adversarial situations.

CHAPTER 8

Confrontation planning

Knowing is understanding

Depending on how well you know your colleagues, you may be able to anticipate the amount of resistance you are up against. Consider what action you are going to take before you speak. Keep a list of possible motivational actions ready to hand if you have to encourage troublesome staff to do things they might not like. When dealing with them, be as flexible as possible. Don't always use the same methods and tactics; if you do, they will anticipate what you are going to do and continue to behave badly. An intransigent attitude from a member of staff could be defeated by a flexible approach from you. It might disarm them and bring about a swift conclusion to the argument.

Communicating with people in general – and especially with challenging individuals – requires tact and diplomacy. Evaluating what works best for you and suits your way of operating is important. Inanimate objects can be dealt with efficiently and in reasonably quick time – for example, it's a lot easier to get authorization for a new piece of computer software than it is to find a replacement member of staff.

128   When dealing with people and their emotions, however, matters cannot be rushed.

Rookie Buster

It's a lot easier to get authorization for a new piece of computer software than it is to find a replacement member of staff.

But there is a pragmatic aspect to dealings with colleagues, staff, your boss and others. How much time should you spend on your troubleshooting strategy? Someone else, perhaps much further up the company hierarchy, will have the ultimate solution to the problem: "Cancel the order," "Close that office," "Stop dealing with that supplier." Until you receive those instructions, though, you should keep on trying. And when co-workers are causing pain and anguish, it costs money. That is why you must work as swiftly as possible to bring about a sensible resolution.

Colleagues, clients, staff and others can be the most difficult people on earth, and one way to keep them in check is to use assertive communication techniques. These are essential when trying to find a solution to issues caused by troublesome people.

Assertiveness techniques

What does assertive behaviour help you to do? It enables you to get into the habit of expressing ideas positively and communicating them in a professional way. Assertive communication helps you to satisfy the needs and wants of the other parties involved, assuming they are calm enough to listen to reason. If you are assertive, you will show that you are able to stand up for yourself without attacking the other person. You are most likely to do this, even in the most awkward of situations,

by making positive statements in an honest and direct way. Statements   129
such as:

- "What I'd suggest we do first is ..."
- "There is a way I can probably help you to ..."
- "I'll check for you that ..."
- "It will help to get to grips with this straight away if you ..."
- "How does that sound to you?"

Rookie Buster

If you are assertive, you will show that you are able to stand up for yourself without attacking the other person.

Show the other side that you are positive, confident and prepared to be proactive on their behalf. This will go a long way towards getting them to calm down or move towards your viewpoint.

Often the aim of your colleagues' aggressive behaviour is quite the opposite. Bad conduct can frequently arise from their desire to prove their superiority, to threaten, or to defend themselves against what they perceive as a threat. These people express their thoughts, feelings and beliefs in unsuitable and inappropriate ways. Even if they are in the right, their openly hostile manner drives potential allies away.

Assertiveness can be interpreted as:

- Appropriate behaviour.
- Self-confidence and self-esteem.
- Willingness to communicate.
- Being positive and proactive.

When you behave assertively, you leave others in no doubt that you are in control, but not controlling. The key to being

130   assertive is that, in any difficult situation, you leave the exchange feeling OK about yourself and the other person involved ("I'm OK, he's OK"). The aim is for a win–win outcome in terms of mutual respect and self-respect. Assertiveness is similar to persuasive communication techniques, but stronger. Communicating in an assertive way, you say what you mean and you mean what you say by giving clear, straightforward messages. You will show that you can:

- Be direct.
- Be appropriate.
- Take responsibility.
- Remain calm and in control.
- Be willing to listen.

If you get your assertiveness technique right, a lot of the anxiety you may feel about facing challenging situations will disappear. Your confidence will grow and you will no longer be timid in potentially confrontational exchanges. Your feelings of guilt, embarrassment and frustration will evaporate. Assertiveness allows you to understand yourself and be who you really are.

Rookie Buster

Assertiveness allows you to understand yourself and be who you really are.

Distinguishing characteristics

The contrast between aggressiveness and assertiveness is marked. An *aggressive* response is a put-down. It is often a personal attack, tinged with sarcasm and arrogance. An *assertive* response is a reasonable objection, delivered in a polite but positive manner. When faced with a difficult situation, an assertive response could require you to postpone tackling the issue. Why does this help? It shows that you have

courage and confidence and are not being railroaded into action   131
without appropriate consideration. It can help you:

- Create a boundary.
- Buy yourself some time.
- Avoid rambling excuses if you don't yet have the facts.

You are being assertive if you refuse to be pushed into a situation
you are not ready to tackle. A confrontational colleague who is revel-
ling in creating a clash of wills should not be given satisfaction. He
may have allowed his "inner child" to escape in the workplace, but you
should remain uninvolved. Resist the temptation to shout back "Oh,
why don't you just grow up?" This won't help, because you will be
behaving in an equally juvenile manner.

Rookie Buster

You are being assertive if you refuse to be pushed into a
situation you are not ready to tackle.

Summoning all your confidence and skill, you should be able to buy
yourself some time. Show no signs of annoyance, sarcasm or arrogance, but allow your voice to register concern and interest for your
difficult colleague. What you are attempting to do here is to deal with
a childish person in an adult manner. With a bit of breathing space,
your colleague may come to his senses. If he does behave more sensi-
bly, you can then begin to deal with the situation (and him) in an adult
way.

Transactional analysis

Underpinning this approach is the theory of transactional analysis
(sometimes known as TA). It was first developed by Eric Berne, an

132   American psychiatrist, who formed his observations of his patients
into a psychological model. This model showed certain patterns of
thought and behaviour. Berne's theory suggests that whatever our age
or status, there are just three ego states from which people operate.
These are parent, adult and child:

- **Parent.** The mixture of behavioural codes that you were brought
  up with during your formative years – the *taught* element.
- **Adult.** The result of the influences on you, your experience of life,
  your perceptions and realizations – the thought element.
- **Child.** This represents how you received those rules which
  surrounded you, the feelings they evoked and how you felt about
  them.

The parent (or teacher) messages are those that usually contain the
"don't", "do", "mind out" and "watch it" words and phrases. This type of
expression tends to lay down rules and give little or no explanation.
These expressions are often critical, so the person to whom they are
addressed feels little and undermined. If you deal with someone by
giving parental messages, you will be telling them they should control
themselves, and that they should not question authority. Perhaps you
are even suggesting they are a nuisance.

The staff member on the receiving
end of this will be the child figure,
being told he or she "should" and
"must" improve, do something
better or quicker, or finish their
work on time. A lot of this conveys
negative messages, and does not
include praise. This is why childish
behaviour at work can be the result
of reprimands that cause employees
to feel bad about themselves. This gets
in the way of them being assertive or positive.

Rookie Buster

Childish behaviour at work can be the result of reprimands that cause employees to feel bad about themselves.

When you communicate with others in the parent ego state, you are most likely to be criticizing them. You probably won't be offering constructive feedback, and will be coming across to them as aggressive: "You shouldn't …", "You've no right …", "You're always …". If these remarks are made to an angry colleague, this will not help. When senior staff at work give out parental messages to their juniors, it causes feelings of humiliation and resentment, and sometimes outright rebelliousness.

Communicating in the parent ego state, your remarks will most likely sound:

- Dominating ("You simply cannot …").
- Inflexible ("You have no choice but to …").
- Patronizing ("When I was in your position …").
- Intimidating ("You'd better sort it out …").
- Commanding ("You will do it …").

This means you aren't being assertive, but aggressive. The person you're dealing with is prevented from being assertive too.

Now, look at things from the child ego state. This is determined by how you felt about things when you were very young. What emotions did you feel: happy, sad, frightened, excited, curious, frustrated, confused, angry, loving, rebellious? You will react to the "parent" remarks with one of these emotions. Children are freely expressive creatures and this is what is not expected in the adult world, particularly in the workplace, where certain emotions should be held in check.

The person who is behaving in a childish way at work is giving way to anger, jealousy and frustration by hitting out at colleagues, superiors or staff. Their behaviour, while spontaneous, is totally selfish. They

134   are showing no regard for the feelings of anyone else. When communicating in a childish way, work colleagues will sound as if they are:

- Moaning ("Why me? It's not fair …").
- Demanding ("I want …").
- Dealing ("I will if you will …").
- Angry (storming out of rooms, slamming doors, etc.).
- Scowling ("It's not my fault …").

When someone at work reacts in an irrational way, they are behaving in their child state. Something sets off that reaction in them – threats, humiliation, frustration or a sense of unfairness.

Rookie Buster

When someone at work reacts in an irrational way, they are behaving in their child state.

The adult ego state is the most desirable one, and the best one from which you can behave assertively. It is the rational approach, created from thought and learned experiences which have made up your character and personality. Your adult state is non-judgemental; it takes account of your own failings and allows other people theirs. This ego state relies on knowledge and learned behaviour. When operating in this state, people behave objectively. People conducting negotiations successfully always operate in the adult ego state. This is why they are able to be assertive and reasonable.

Their remarks may include some of the following:

- Understanding ("I see your argument …").
- Solutionist ("What would you do …").
- Revealing ("It is disappointing to learn …").
- Defining ("So this is how it happened …").

Learning to deal with people from the adult ego state will enable you to develop your assertiveness skills. There is no need to completely suppress the other ego states, as long as you use them wisely. The parent state should be used to show dangers and opportunities. The child state will reflect your experiences throughout life – your emotional responses. Being aware of the three ego states should help you to acknowledge your own behaviour and that of others. If you can work out which ego state someone is in, it will help you decide why it is, or isn't, appropriate for the situation you are currently dealing with. It will also show you why you behave towards some people in a certain way. Assertiveness is having respect for yourself and others.

Rookie Buster

Learning to deal with people from the adult ego state will enable you to develop your assertiveness skills.

New ideas and approaches

Check that your behaviour is positive. What if one of your team came up with an idea for tackling a situation in a particular way? Whether or not you initially think the suggestion might be flawed, don't respond with a remark like "What a ridiculous idea, that'll never work." At a stroke you will have crushed a potential ally, caused the person humiliation and probably forced them to behave aggressively towards you at the next exchange. New ideas are delicate things and they require a response that is from the adult ego state. They can be dealt a terminal blow by an ill-judged remark. What is worse, due to anxiety they may never be aired, or even see the light of day. Have you ever decided to bite your tongue and say nothing because of fear of rejection and humiliation? Would your idea perhaps have saved a situation from getting worse, or brought about helpful changes in your organization?

136

Rookie Buster

New ideas are delicate things and they require a response that is from the adult ego state.

New approaches and ideas are the fuel that companies need to keep them up to date and ahead of their competitors. Never be afraid to air them. If you have a wise boss, he will encourage innovative ideas from his staff, department and team. Not every new idea will be welcomed with open arms, of course. But don't worry about this, and don't take it personally. Resist falling back into the child ego state. Many people fear change, and new things don't always work out ideally. With positive encouragement and open minds, though, discussion can sometimes lead to an unacceptable idea being adapted and then adopted. It could even bring about a better solution than had first been anticipated.

If you have a suggestion to make which could solve a potentially confrontational situation, think about it first, before opening your mouth. It may be that you simply wait a few moments before speaking out at a meeting. If you think it is a particularly strong idea, test it out on a trusted colleague first. Maybe your idea needs a bit more development. It is always sensible to consider both the short-term and the long-term implications of the solution. Your idea might for example rectify one aspect of the dispute, but cause wider ranging effects in other departments.

Rookie Buster

If you have a suggestion to make which could solve a potentially confrontational situation, think about it first, before opening your mouth.

Give it some consideration first, and then, if you decide it is worth 137 putting forward as a potential solution, make the suggestion with conviction and confidence. If it is not taken up, don't worry. It may not have been the right time, or you may not yet have reached the point where you are recognized as a "new ideas" person. Saying "May I make a suggestion?" politely and appropriately is usually viewed as helpful. Your colleagues, boss and staff will be grateful that you have given thinking time to their predicament.

Coach's notes

Never personalize a difference of opinion. Listen impartially to the exchange and try to find out if a particular behaviour pattern is dominant. Do not react instinctively. When responding, focus on what was said, not on the way the person behaved. Whether you are dealing with an aggrieved person or the suspected aggressor, retain an objective stance. Where you have to disagree with a colleague, a neutral comment is more likely to be accepted. As long as they haven't behaved appallingly badly, you could thank them for their contribution to the exchange. This could completely disarm them, and the discussion can then be continued without rancour.

Go for it! If you observe people at work, try to work out when they are in their "adult" "parent" or "child" ego states. How many "parents" and "children" are there in your department? A solution to a confrontational exchange is more likely to be reached when both parties are communicating in the adult mode. People who behave in an assertive way are "adults".

Winning people over is another way of dealing with awkward characters. Previous chapters have already dealt with conflict situations, challenging personalities and problem solving. Is it possible that there are ways of charming people out of their moods? What price a little praise? Using honey instead of vinegar with difficult people can sometimes work. But remember, there's a great difference between giving praise to win support and improve attitudes among colleagues and staff, and paying someone a compliment because you wish to gain their friendship. Be sure in your own mind what purpose lies behind your actions. Otherwise you'll confuse not only yourself but everyone else as well.

CHAPTER 9

Charm them, don't alarm them

The fragile balance

Is it possible to mix work and friendship? Friendships at work can be helpful and useful, spreading a feel-good factor across the office. Everyone benefits from a pleasant working environment. If nothing else, you spend a good deal of time there, and without friendly faces an office can be a fairly bleak place. Chatting with colleagues and bonding with team members help to make people feel they belong. But the foundations of such friendships can be fragile.

One of the reasons office friendships aren't easy is because they can be deceptive. You may have worked with someone for a long time, spending most of each day with them for months at a time – possibly even years. You've learned a great deal about them, yet, once you leave work, do your paths ever cross? If you happened to meet one evening, each of you with a group of your personal friends, would you feel you wanted to join up? Would your instant reaction be to move away to the other side of the room, and hope to avoid eye contact? What if, after a number of years working alongside each other, you left for another job? Would you stay friends even though you no longer worked together?

Professional friendships are at the mercy of other factors, such as promotion, preferment and competition. The one who does not share the same amount of success could feel "used" by the other party. Under such circumstances it is likely that the friendship would wither, and this is going to be difficult. Should something actually go wrong with the friendship itself, it is more awkward. A colleague who feels slighted, betrayed or victimized can become a dangerous adversary. Someone with shaky self-confidence, thwarted ambitions, buried prejudices and jealousies is like a simmering volcano. Add sexual tensions to the mix (and few work environments are without them) and the situation can be lethal. Sometimes you may try to feign friendship just to avoid any falling out. This is fraught with difficulty, but it is perhaps necessary to avoid any animosity or hostility breaking out and spreading across the department.

Rookie Buster

Professional friendships are at the mercy of other factors, such as promotion, preferment and competition.

There are two courses of action. The first is to avoid all friendships at work. Remain amicable towards everyone, but go no further than the acquaintance level. The second is to be completely honest in all your dealings with people. If you're honest about the reason for your friendships, you can enjoy them for what they are. People spend so much time at work, there is evidence that many personal relationships in fact begin with an office friendship. The most important thing is to be genuine and sincere. Don't flatter just to get some personal benefit. Admiration for others is a natural instinct, and character is more important than professional status. You don't need to be friends with everyone. Your colleagues may have differing views to yours, and they are entitled to them. Be professional in your dealings, and treat colleagues politely at first. Make friends with people when you know them and because you like them, not because of the position they occupy.

Rookie Buster

Make friends with people when you know them and because you like them, not because of the position they occupy.

Popularity at work is worth aiming for. If you are accepted by colleagues, co-workers, staff and the management hierarchy, it will significantly influence the atmosphere in which you work. It is important to preserve people's dignity and respect wherever possible. This alone could reduce the number of difficult situations you might have to deal with. Someone who rides roughshod over other people's feelings in the workplace does end up facing trouble – mainly caused by his or her own actions.

It's not a sign of failure to admit there are some people you simply can't win over. But if you are prepared to try the charm method, practise the use of non-verbal communication to soften the hard-line position of others:

S (smile)
O (open posture)
F (forward looking)
T (touch)
E (eye contact)
N (nod)

If you approach someone with a smile, it will encourage a similar response from them. Just as important is your presentation and body language. The posture should be open, head upright, and you should stand straight but with hands relaxed by your sides. Make appropriate gestures to show that you are welcoming the exchange. If it is helpful, shake hands. Should a meeting be taking place, gesture where to sit or what room is to be used. Eye contact should be honest and open. Avoid staring, but maintain a steady gaze when speaking to your colleague.

144   At the same time, encourage him by nodding your head to show consensus, or indicate that you are taking note of the points he is making. If you are giving the right signals, he may mirror your actions.

Praise not blame

Is your workplace known as a hotbed of intrigue, backstabbing and politicking? Do harassment, bullying and discrimination take place? Do reports and complaints regularly get made to the HR department? Unfortunately there are some organizations which have just such a reputation. And sometimes an atmosphere worsens when a new arrival joins the company. Maybe someone's approach needs a makeover? It is easier to adapt an individual's manner when dealing with others than it is to alter an endemic organizational culture.

    Good helpings of praise go down well in the workplace. No matter how often motivational consultants dream up extravagant reward schemes and exotic incentive trips for staff, this isn't the only formula for success. One of the keys to retaining staff is to let them know they are appreciated. It creates a strong sense of camaraderie amongst them. The more staff feel valued and are given some control over how, when and where their job is done, the happier they will be. Their performance improves, along with their morale. There is less confrontational behaviour – in short, everyone gains.

Rookie Buster

The more staff feel valued and are given some control over how, when and where their job is done, the happier they will be.

Regardless of how advanced technology has become and what the latest equipment and gadgets enable us to do, some things are in danger of becoming too impersonal and remote. There is something very encouraging about good manners and personal attention. When the workplace is plagued by bad behaviour or bad manners, there is bound to be an increase in resignations and absence for sick leave.

Sweet success

Kindness goes a long way too. If someone among your colleagues is showing signs of anxiety, stress or depression, they are probably feeling inadequate and undervalued. If left unchecked, this situation could spiral towards absenteeism. You should be aware of work-related anxiety and its effects. There is a marked difference between stress and anxiety – the former is caused by overstimulation and overload, while the latter is usually the result of the person feeling a failure, a poor performer or inadequate. And if this person is the victim of bullying, harassment, sexual or racial prejudice, they could suffer from a number of physical symptoms – shortness of breath, nervous behaviour, back-ache or headaches, eating disorders and insomnia.

Rookie Buster

If someone among your colleagues is showing signs of anxiety, stress or depression, they are probably feeling inadequate and undervalued.

Although dealing with anxiety is best done by seeking professional help, kindness can go a long way to combat its effects. Helping your colleague cope with challenging situations by praising them will allevi-ate some symptoms. Come up with some positive statements that will encourage your colleague to stop thinking that they can't cope. If they are stressed because they are unable to deal with authority, they may feel powerless to do anything about it. Helping them to understand why the rules are there and that it's not a personal issue will prevent them becoming hostile. Remind them they are not alone and that you are willing to offer them support. Just as people who come from safe, stable backgrounds are less likely to suffer anxiety-related problems, if you can encourage staff to feel that the workplace is a safe environment, this will have a positive effect on them.

Should you be required to deliver some criticism to someone who is under-performing, it is possible to do so without hurting their feelings. Be positive, and explain that you want to help them. Have the conversation with them at an appropriate time and place, so as to avoid embarrassing them in public, particularly if it is a sensitive issue. You need to be sure that the person knows what you are talking about – whether it is their performance over the past few months or a piece of work they have delivered to you that morning. Be specific and keep it concise: for example, "Your poor timekeeping is causing a problem for the department." Reminding them that they have been a great role model in the past will reinforce their identity and encourage them to think positively about themselves.

Motivation

Keeping people's motivation high and not allowing grumpiness to pervade the office is one of the many challenges you may face. Being happy around them should help to encourage a warmer atmosphere. Beware of the chill factor: don't allow moody people to simmer, as this contaminates the workplace swiftly. It is much easier to work with good-tempered colleagues. The difficult will find it much harder to be cross if you're nice to them. If you write a personal note of thanks to someone, this is an effective way of increasing their morale and self-esteem. It is rare to get a hand-written message, and what it conveys is that the recipient is worthy of respect.

It is a sign that someone is confident if they project a warm, encouraging expression. When a smile lights up your face, people will notice you. Imagine the powerful advantage this gives you in a potential conflict situation. People who smile give the impression of being pleasant, attractive, sincere and confident. This relaxes the person with whom you are about to communicate.

147

Rookie Buster

If you write a personal note of thanks to someone, this is an effective way of increasing their morale and self-esteem.

A conflict can be resolved or a relationship enhanced purely through a display of confidence. Self-belief and self-assurance are vital if you are to realize your potential and maximize your success in dealing with challenging individuals. But confidence – like a muscle – needs to be exercised if it is to develop.

One of the bonuses of giving praise is that it stops most people complaining. Whiners can be a nuisance at work. If they are managed properly you can move them away from moaning. If you are determined to eradicate troublemakers from your department, you should spend time with some of the moaners. Discover if there are genuine

148 grievances which need proper examination, or just niggling issues which can be sorted out fairly easily.

Negative perspectives can be pernicious. If there are a number of people making waves within a department, this is where the rot can set in. You cannot afford to have a vicious circle of miserable people fuelling their own gloomy forebodings. You could help yourself and your company by planning and promoting an "anti-whinging" strategy. The effect is to allow the moaners to rant and rave about what upsets them, on condition that once they have had their say, they will take part in a motivational exercise and be willing to approach new ideas and develop their implementation. This approach helps the grumblers to feel they are being taken seriously, which raises their morale and self-esteem. Setting them a series of meaningful goals will instil confidence and strength in them. One step at a time is usually enough to help these people change. But the most important factor in all this is praising and rewarding even the smallest amount of success or progress.

Rookie Buster

The most important factor is praising and rewarding even the smallest amount of success or progress.

There can be failures, such as when problems are deep rooted. Part of any managerial challenge is to motivate employees so that they overcome barriers of every kind. They should not be allowed to lose faith in their organization or their own future prospects. Unhappy employees aren't converted swiftly, but with encouragement and praise they can be developed. Corporate cultures should offer respect and dignity to all employees. Temper that with some praise and reward, and much can be achieved.

Dealing with professional jealousy 149

However persistent you are, not everyone will love you. Professional jealousy can thrive in the workplace, and this requires careful handling. You may be doing really well in your job, but others may not, in which case you could face envy and resentment, rather than encouragement and support from your colleagues. Job jealousy is not unusual, and many people feel that their colleagues are trying to undermine their success or block their progress.

One reason for professional jealousy is feeling threatened. Is someone at work feeling resentful towards you because of your recent promotion? Or is it because you are popular and polished and they are not? Some people regard work as a competition with only one winner. Should you be seen to be edging closer to the chequered flag, they may see you as winning and themselves as losing. The only way they can deal with this is to push themselves forward and hold you back at the same time. Professional jealousy can take many forms – from the odd "forgotten" message or mislaid written instruction, to a formal request for information which fails to get delivered. Should you feel that your work is being undermined or criticized unfairly, you will need to make a note of such things.

Focus on what is important and ignore what is trivial. If you want to bask in self-congratulation, don't do it in the workplace. Celebrate your success outside among friends. Jealous colleagues are out to make life difficult for you. You need to maintain your own standards, rather than dropping them to their level. You may have to be brave and tackle the person out in the open. Confront him or her and say you have something on your mind which needs to be discussed. Your request for a chat will probably be refused, in which case ask whether this is just a bad time, and would they suggest a better time?

 **Rookie Buster**

Focus on what is important and ignore what is trivial.

Don't be put off by them, but persist until they agree to talk to you. You could open the conversation by saying that you feel there is a bit of tension between you and you wonder if everything is alright. If they say, "I've no idea what you're talking about," then you can say, "Oh good, I must have been mistaken. I'm glad because I want us to be able to work together." Make it clear that if they have something they wish to discuss in future, they must say so. It is important that the exchange concludes on a positive note, so that both parties can exit with some dignity.

Should matters not improve, you will have to set up another one-to-one exchange at which you are more assertive. Spell out the point of grievance – for example, "It is not acceptable when you do x. I find it difficult working with you. Please make sure that in future you do y. Are you OK with this?" Unfortunately, if this doesn't work you have no choice but to make a complaint along formal lines. Disciplinary action may follow, but since there is little chance of you establishing trust and rapport with this work colleague, there is no other option. Whatever you do, you must stay professional. The most important thing is to work through this difficulty if at all possible without creating problems for others in the department.

Coach's notes

From the advice in this chapter you should be able to decide when it is worth putting on kid gloves and dealing with people softly. It doesn't always work, but sometimes it is useful to know how to use soft tactics as well as tough ones. Being sympathetic to people, praising them, motivating them and encouraging them, can alleviate departmental tantrums, moans and groans. There are times when being nice to people doesn't work, but you should make your own decision as to what sort of treatment is appropriate and when and then carry it out confidently.

Go for it! Charm, good manners, politeness – these are sometimes in short supply due to pressure of work. But if you can cultivate courtesy towards others, it should win you friends and influence people. It is always a good idea to approach people mildly at first. They are less likely to react angrily if you are pleasant to them and if other people in the department are behaving well.

Notes

As technology progresses, does human interaction matter more or less? Global conflict, global warming, economic crises, financial insta-bility – with all of this unfolding, how likely is it that people are going to manage live peaceably together? So what are the chances of main-taining harmonious workplace relationships? This chapter recaps on the previous chapters and offers suggestions for continuing good practice in keeping the workplace as healthy an environment as possible.

CHAPTER 10

Future perfect?

Keeping control

Will new discoveries and advancing technology enable people to cope better with each other? Scientific progress allows people to live and work under the sea, underground, on land and in space. Encouraging harmonious societies and groupings is necessary to avoid extinction. Communication networks make it possible to transmit, store, process and output information at ever-growing speed.

If people used their brains to their full potential they might not have difficulty in dealing with the infinitely varied characters they co-exist with. Everyone learns from experience. Each person is constantly making judgements of one kind or another. People's greatest ability is the capacity for reflective thought – the knowledge that you know something. Humans have this unique cognitive ability, but they don't always employ it when dealing with each other. How much time do people spend actually working out what makes others behave they way they do?

Rookie Buster

How much time do people spend actually working out what makes others behave they way they do?

Much of the technology everyone will be using in the next ten years has already been invented. It just needs further research and development. With scientific and technological progress, people will live longer. There will be even more time to argue, complain and irritate each other. The challenge everyone faces in the 21st century is twofold: learning to live with advancing technology, and learning to cope with each other.

Those in power need to look long and hard at how social behaviour is changing. Today every business is increasingly aware that it should exercise corporate social responsibility (or CSR). Companies adopting this policy of responsible behaviour create a code of conduct among employees. Corporate social responsibility assumes that companies should be accountable not only for their financial performance, but also for ethical issues, including the impact of their activities on society and on the environment. Striking this balance is all-important.

Businesses are already accountable for areas that are generally embraced by CSR, such as human resources, environmental issues, sustainable development, waste management and health and safety practices. In business, financial imperatives force many confrontational relationships to evolve into collaborative ones. Past competitors may well become partners, working together to survive in the global market. Are individuals likely to learn from examples like this how to behave better towards each other? Powerful people make decisions that have far-reaching implications for many others. Decisiveness with flexibility is key. Pushing on with a flawed decision and pouring effort and resources into a failing project rarely provide a satisfactory solution. In such situations, remember that confrontation exacerbates the problem; collaboration is what is needed.

Rookie Buster

Pushing on with a flawed decision and pouring effort and resources into a failing project rarely provide a satisfactory solution.

When society was based on agricultural or agrarian culture, it was a matter of survive and thrive together, or perish divided. Communities flourished if everyone worked together in a harmonious fashion. Today, in our very different high-tech, high-speed age, it will similarly only be through employers, clients and colleagues working together that better results will be achieved for everyone.

Discipline

Now that you have nearly reached the end of the final chapter, here is a summary of tactics for dealing with difficult people:

1. If someone behaves unreasonably at work and it's a one-off, perhaps a gentle reminder is all that's required. But if it keeps happening, morale plummets and you must act.

2. Everyone in the workplace is entitled to be treated with dignity and respect. Bullying, harassment and discrimination should not be tolerated. Companies should have policies and procedures for dealing with grievance and disciplinary matters. Check that yours is in place and up to date with regard to current employment law.

3. If you need to take action, you must be clear about what steps are involved. Disciplining staff should

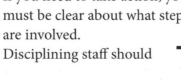

158   not be confused with punishment. Discipline is positive; punishing someone is to do with exacting a penalty. Disciplining an employee can be an informal or formal procedure, depending on the severity of the problem.

4. Set a good example by dealing with an issue fast. Maintain fair procedures, and set standards of behaviour by means of an organizational policy issued to all staff. There is a clear distinction between issues related to performance and misconduct. Be sure you identify the problem.

Attitude

And here's a checklist of how to maintain a positive attitude at work:

1. Train your brain to accept only the messages you want to accept. Don't allow it to absorb negative information.
2. When faced with a problem, look for a solution, not a reason to give up. Remember – you only fail when you quit.
3. The central nervous system cannot tell the difference between a real and an imagined event. If you can convince your subconscious of what you want, you will instinctively start taking the actions that will make it happen for you.
4. Problems that you can overcome become positive experiences. Consider what you can learn from things that have turned out differently to your original expectations.

Accepting change

Embrace change. Change happens, and there's not much you can do about it. Some people ignore it; others try to stop it. If you are dealing with difficult people at work, maybe they are fighting the inevitable and resisting change.

There are four phases through which people pass before they embrace change. These are:

- *Denial.* "That's never going to work," or "We tried that already."

Do you recognize the ostriches in your organization? They may have their heads in the sand, but change is not going to go away as a result of their not seeing it.

- *Resistance.* Some people try to stick with the old ways of doing things: "But it's always worked OK in the past." The reality is, the sooner you get to grips with the new system, the better it is for your career (and your blood pressure).

- *Exploration.* Maybe the change doesn't have to be all bad. Is it possible that there are some advantages to the new way of working? If you look at the change with a more open mind, you may begin to find some good things that come from it.

- *Acceptance.* Once you reach this stage, you may even find that the new systems works better than you'd believed possible. You have by this time fully integrated the change into your own routine.

Coach's notes

There are a number of things people do to cause difficulty at work:
- Use old methods of working when they should be playing by the new rules.
- Avoid taking on new assignments for fear that they might have to work in a different way.
- Try to slow things down to their own pace. Unfortunately change usually requires people to speed up, so they risk getting left further and further behind.
- Play the victim/martyr role. Unfortunately, more flexible colleagues won't show them any sympathy.
- Try to control the uncontrollable. This is a bit like attempting to stop the tide from coming on to the beach. Change is inevitable – they'll have to accept it. Instead of wasting energy resisting, they should just go with the flow.

You may be working with a number of colleagues whose behaviour is similar to that described above. Their difficulty lies in their entrenched attitude. Don't allow yourself to resist change. If you can show your employers that you are willing to embrace it, they will quickly realize what an incredible asset you are to the organization. You're a survivor, and your responsiveness to change will be your passport to future success.

If you can position yourself within your organization as someone with the right attitude, able to embrace change, who wants to help others, you will be seen to be outward looking. Develop strengths such as:
- Reliability.
- Honesty.
- Integrity.
- Patience.

Research has proved that people with successful personal relationships are happier, healthier and live longer. Those who can coexist peaceably at work suffer less stress and gain more workplace satisfaction. To be successful at dealing with people, and enjoying harmonious relationships with them, you need to learn to respect and trust them. Then allow them time to do the same for you. This is why the ability to deal with difficult people and build healthy workplace relationships is a beneficial skill, not just for you and your colleagues, but for future generations too.

Go for it! A person who successfully relates to others and can deal sympathetically with difficult colleagues is a valuable asset to any organization. This type of person doesn't waste time learning how to talk, but instead learns how to listen. Take the time to understand the different needs of those around you. If you don't, colleagues can become increasingly demanding or disgruntled. It works both ways: if your colleagues couldn't care less where you stand, it will make you feel worthless and unimportant. Everyone wants to be valued and appreciated, and it is this professional approach to workplace relationships that will bring success.

Notes

Index